FLOYD CLYMER'S MOTORCYCLIST'S LIBRARY

The Book of the
NORTON

A PRACTICAL GUIDE ON THE HANDLING AND MAINTENANCE OF ALL 1955-63 O.H.V. SINGLE-CYLINDER TOURING TYPE NORTONS

BY

W. C. HAYCRAFT
F.R.S.A.

ANNOUNCEMENT

By special arrangement with the original publishers of this book, Sir Isaac Pitman & Son, Ltd., of London, England, we have secured the exclusive publishing rights for this book, as well as all others in THE MOTORCYCLIST'S LIBRARY.

Included in THE MOTORCYCLIST'S LIBRARY are complete instruction manuals covering the care and operation of respective motorcycles and engines; valuable data on speed tuning, and thrilling accounts of motorcycle race events. See listing of available titles elsewhere in this edition.

We consider it a privilege to be able to offer so many fine titles to our customers.

FLOYD CLYMER
Publisher of Books Pertaining to Automobiles and Motorcycles

2125 W. PICO ST.   LOS ANGELES 6, CALIF.

INTRODUCTION

Welcome to the world of digital publishing ~ the book you now hold in your hand, while unchanged from the original edition, was printed using the latest state of the art digital technology. The advent of print-on-demand has forever changed the publishing process, never has information been so accessible and it is our hope that this book serves your informational needs for years to come. If this is your first exposure to digital publishing, we hope that you are pleased with the results. Many more titles of interest to the classic automobile and motorcycle enthusiast, collector and restorer are available via our website at www.VelocePress.com. We hope that you find this title as interesting as we do.

NOTE FROM THE PUBLISHER

The information presented is true and complete to the best of our knowledge. All recommendations are made without any guarantees on the part of the author or the publisher, who also disclaim all liability incurred with the use of this information.

TRADEMARKS

We recognize that some words, model names and designations, for example, mentioned herein are the property of the trademark holder. We use them for identification purposes only. This is not an official publication.

INFORMATION ON THE USE OF THIS PUBLICATION

This manual is an invaluable resource for the classic motorcycle enthusiast and a "must have" for owners interested in performing their own maintenance. However, in today's information age we are constantly subject to changes in common practice, new technology, availability of improved materials and increased awareness of chemical toxicity. As such, it is advised that the user consult with an experienced professional prior to undertaking any procedure described herein. While every care has been taken to ensure correctness of information, it is obviously not possible to guarantee complete freedom from errors or omissions or to accept liability arising from such errors or omissions. Therefore, any individual that uses the information contained within, or elects to perform or participate in do-it-yourself repairs or modifications acknowledges that there is a risk factor involved and that the publisher or its associates cannot be held responsible for personal injury or property damage resulting from the use of the information or the outcome of such procedures.

WARNING!

One final word of advice, this publication is intended to be used as a reference guide, and when in doubt the reader should consult with a qualified technician.

PREFACE

THE author has aimed at providing a *readable* book of reference (for novices and experts), and has spared no pains to make it as complete as possible. He has in preparing the MS. derived a pleasure second only to that which actual Norton riding experience has given him.

The products of Norton Motors Ltd., Plumstead Rd., Woolwich, London, S.E. 18 (WOOlwich 1223) need no introduction. Their stamina, power, reliability, and tenacious road holding are renowned everywhere and have been amply demonstrated by famous riders such as Duke, Amm, Daniell, Woods, Guthrie, and Frith.

The present edition of this handbook contains *all* essential maintenance and stripping-down instructions for the following overhead-valve single-cylinder Nortons—

1. The 1955–8 596 c.c. Model 19
2. The 1955–62 490 c.c. Model ES2
3. The 1956–62 348 c.c. Model 50

Instructions not dated in this handbook apply to all 1955 and later spring frame four-stroke single-cylinder models. The following machines are not covered: the Trials, and all twin-cylinder models. The 1962 Models 50 and ES2 remain unchanged for 1963 and therefore all maintenance instructions for these models apply also to 1963.

I thank Norton Motors Ltd., for assistance in regard to technical data, and for according me permission to reproduce various Norton copyright illustrations. I am also grateful to some accessory firms for their helpful co-operation. Finally, I wish all Norton owners maximum trouble-free mileage at minimum cost.

W. C. H.

CONTENTS

I. HANDLING A NORTON 1
   Preliminaries—Use of controls

II. LUCAS DYNAMO LIGHTING (1955-8 MODELS) . . . 10
   Dynamo maintenance—Care of the Lucas battery—The Lucas lamps—Bulb renewal—The lighting switch and horn—Wiring diagrams

III. THE LIGHTING AND IGNITION SYSTEM (1959-62 MODELS) . . 24

IV. LUBRICATION 32
   Engine lubrication—The motor-cycle parts

V. THE AMAL CARBURETTOR 40
   How it works (1955 onwards)—Tuning the carburettor—Maintenance

VI. GENERAL MAINTENANCE 50
   Tools, etc.—Sparking plugs and the Lucas "Magdyno"—Valve clearances—Decarbonizing engine—Ignition and valve timing—Hints on engine overhaul—The transmission—Wheels, brakes, and tyres—Steering head adjustment—Telescopic forks and rear Springing.

Index 121

CHAPTER 1

HANDLING A NORTON

IT is assumed that you have bought a brand new or a second-hand Norton. If you are a complete novice, there are a number of points with which you must become fully conversant before taking to the road. Obtain and read carefully a copy of the latest edition of the *Highway Code*. Buy and wear a reliable crash helmet.

The Riding Position. If this is not entirely satisfactory, it is possible to make a combined adjustment of the handlebars, handlebar controls, and footrests. The handlebars can readily be adjusted after slackening the securing bolts, and clip fittings enable the positions of the handlebar levers to be varied. The shafts for the footrest hangers and the shaft for the gear-change pedal are on most machines serrated and splined respectively, and an appreciable variation in the position of the footrests and pedal is possible.

With the riding position correct, the body should be nicely balanced and poised slightly forwards, with the arms practically straight and the hands gently resting on the handlebar grips. The angle between the thighs and the lower parts of the legs should be very slightly less than a right-angle and the rear of the sole should rest comfortably on each footrest, with the toe in such a position that upward and downward gear changes can be made without moving the foot from the footrest.

USE OF CONTROLS

Layout and Handling. The layout of the controls on 1955–62 O.H.V. Nortons is shown in Figs. 1–3. Controls fall into two groups: (1) engine controls, and (2) motor-cycle controls. If you are a complete novice, sit on the saddle of your mount, and "twiddle" the various levers while meditating on what the effect would be if the engine were running. Those handling a Norton for the first time should note the following—

1. All handlebar controls (including the throttle twist-grip) are operated by *inward* movement.

2. The throttle twist-grip (which controls engine speed) has a full movement of approximately *one-quarter* of a complete turn. With the throttle-stop correctly set to provide good tick-over, the throttle slide does not close completely. On most Nortons it is essential to use a very small throttle opening (about one-sixteenth to one-eighth of an inch as measured

1

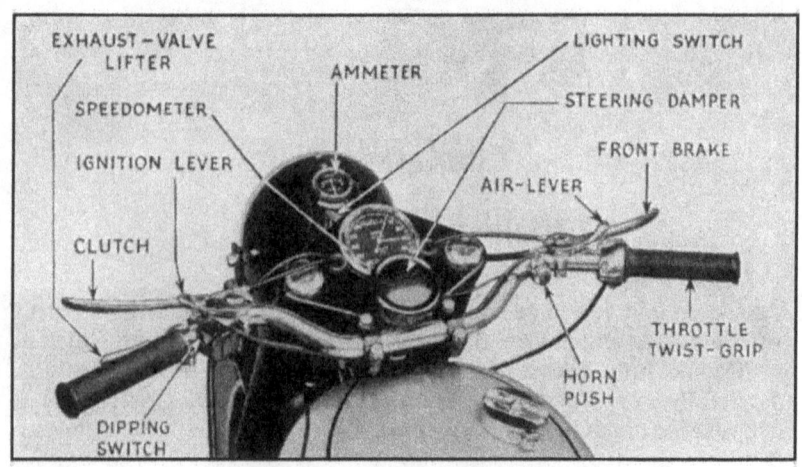

Fig. 1. The Control Layout (1955 Models)

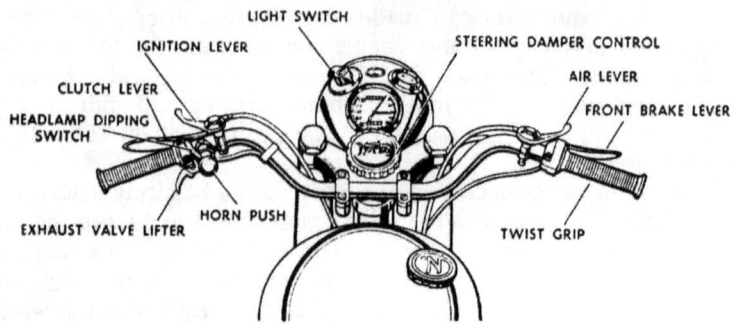

Fig. 2. The Control Layout (1956–8 Models)

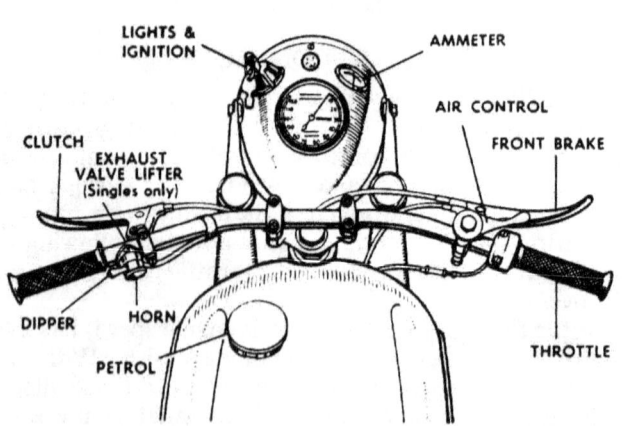

Fig. 3. The Control Layout (1959–62 Models)

at the rim of the twist-grip rubber) for starting purposes, otherwise some difficulty may be experienced in making a start.

3. The air lever (which enables the mixture of air and petrol to be varied) must be kept closed completely for starting from *cold* but at all other times it should normally be *wide open*. Slight closing when travelling slowly under load, to ward off a tendency for pinking, may sometimes be desirable, but it is generally best to use the ignition lever to forestall pinking.

4. The ignition lever (which moves the contact-breaker base on the magneto portion of a "Magdyno" should always be kept fully, or nearly fully, advanced while riding, except when pinking occurs. Then the ignition should be temporarily retarded a shade, but note that this automatically reduces the power output. At the first opportunity after temporary retardation, the ignition lever should be *advanced as far as possible*. For starting purposes, however, it is always advisable to retard the ignition lever to at least the half-way position.

5. All 1959–62 Nortons have coil instead of magneto ignition. An ignition key is provided on the top of the lighting and ignition switch. For all normal starting and riding the key should be turned in a *clockwise* direction to the IGN position. For emergency starting, however, the key should be turned in an *anti-clockwise* direction to the EMG position. (*see* page 25.) When parking a Norton always turn the ignition key to the OFF position and remove it from the switch.

6. Never use the exhaust-valve lifter (which raises the exhaust valve off its seat) for any purpose other than starting and stopping the engine. It is permissible, however, to use it occasionally when descending hills, provided that the throttle is shut right back and the air lever is wide open.

7. The clutch lever (which disconnects and reconnects the drive from the engine to the rear wheel) must always be used *fully* and *progressively*. Use it only when moving off and during each gear change.

8. The foot gear-change pedal on the off-side of the gearbox provides four gear ratios and "neutral" which lies between first and second gears. Note that "neutral" should only be obtained *after* engaging first gear. All downward changes (*see* Fig. 5) are made by upward movement of the pedal with the toe, and all upward changes are made by downward movement of the pedal with the toe. The gear-change pedal returns to the same (horizontal) position after each gear change is effected, ready for the next change to be made. During each gear change it is necessary to make a *full* movement of the gear-change pedal.

Fuel and Oil Replenishment. It is beneficial with O.H.V. engines, especially during the running-in period, to add a little upper-cylinder lubricant to the petrol each time the tank is replenished. Suitable lubricants are Redex, Castrollo, Mixtrol, B.P. Energol UCL, Filtrate Colloidal Petroyle, etc. Liquid lubricant is preferable to that in tablet form, and the container cap is often employed as a measure. Alternatively the garage hand will inject one or two "shots" after tanking up with petrol.

The Norton fuel tank (capacity: 1959–62 models, $3\frac{1}{2}$ gal; 1956–8 models, $3\frac{1}{4}$ gal) has at its base a decent-size gauze filter, but never neglect to use a funnel with a filter when replenishing from a can, as impurities are apt to form a sediment at the tank bottom and interfere with free supply to the engine, due to the tank filter becoming clogged.

Always replenish the oil tank with the correct brand and grade of oil recommended by Norton Motors Ltd. (*see* Chapter IV). Before checking the oil level, run the engine a few minutes to scavenge the sump. The oil level in the tank should not be more than three-quarters full and should never be allowed to fall below the half-full level in the tank.

If the oil level is below the half-full mark (the minimum oil level is marked on the outside of the tank), the insufficient oil in circulation tends to overheat. If the tank is topped up too high, pressure built up inside the tank by the oil return pipe will force surplus oil through the air-release pipe on to the road.

Norton Motors Ltd., recommend the addition of some running-in compound (containing "colloidal graphite") to the *engine oil* during the running-in period. The usual proportions to use are *one pint* of running-in compound to each gallon of oil, but if use of the compound is continued after running-in, the quantity added should be halved.

Always Maintain Correct Tyre Pressures. The pressures should be checked weekly. Suitable pressure gauges are the Dunlop No. 6, Holdtite, Romac, and Schrader No. 7750. To use a gauge, the valve dust cap (Fig. 4) is taken off, and the end of the pressure gauge is pressed on to the open end of the valve. It depresses the pin and allows air to enter the gauge and push up the piston calibrated in pounds per square inch. Always keep the dust caps screwed on firmly! Dust or grit getting into the valve stem is liable to interfere with the valve action of the little spring-controlled plunger (Fig. 4) and cause leakage. About once a year valve "insides" should be replaced. They can be removed by taking off the valve cap and using the slotted end as a screwdriver.

Correct solo tyre pressures for 3·25 in. × 19 in. front and rear tyres fitted to 1955–58 Model 19 Nortons are 22 lb per sq in. and 25 lb per sq in. respectively. Correct solo front and rear tyre pressures for 1955–58 Models ES2 and 50 with 3·25 in. × 19 in. front and rear tyres are 23 lb per sq in. and 20 lb per sq in.

In the case of 1959 Models ES2 and 50 with 3·00 in. × 19 in. and 3·5 in. × 19 in. front and rear tyres the correct solo tyre pressures are 25 lb per sq in. and 20 lb per sq in. respectively.

On 1960–62 Models ES2 and 50 with 3·00 in. × 19 in. and 3·50 in. × 19 in. front and rear tyres the correct solo pressures are 25 lb per sq in. and 22 lb per sq in. respectively.

Note that where heavy luggage or a pillion passenger is carried it is desirable to increase the pressure of the rear tyre by several lb per sq in.

Setting Controls for Starting Up (1955 Onwards). First make sure that there is sufficient oil of the correct grade in the oil tank, gearbox, and oil-bath chain case (*see* Chapter IV), and that the various motor-cycle parts have been properly lubricated. The oil tank holds four pints (*see* page 4). Also check that the tyre pressures are correct (*see* previous paragraph), and that there is sufficient petrol in the tank. Pull your Norton backward

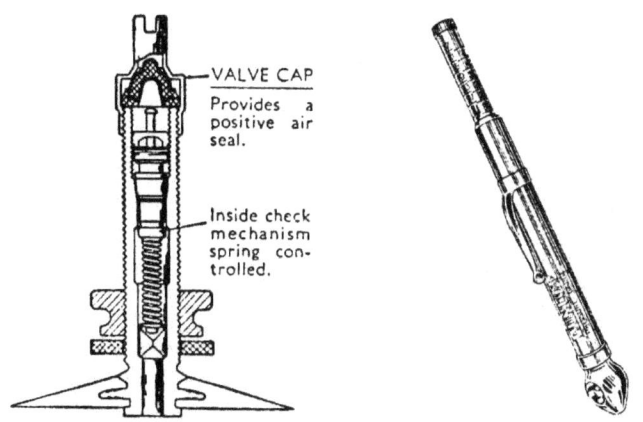

Fig. 4. Showing (Left) Dunlop Valve and (Right) Dunlop No. 6 Pocket Pressure Gauge

on to its spring-up centre stand and prepare to start up. Note that when attempting to start up with the machine off its stand, it is advisable to stand astride the machine, as this helps to balance it. On a 1955–9 Norton with a single reserve petrol tap, verify that the reserve tap (the off-side one) is turned off, and turn on the main tap. To turn on the tap, press the hexagonal button; to turn off, press the knurled button. On machines with two taps either tap may be used as a reserve, and will provide fuel for 5–8 miles running. Most later Nortons (1959–62) have a single two-positional reserve tap. Prior to starting up, pull out the knurled circular knob. Should the reserve supply be required, the knob must be turned and pulled out a further amount.

To obtain a quick start, it is important to set the controls correctly. Verify that the foot gear-change pedal is in the "neutral" position, i.e. between first and second gears (*see* Fig. 5). Make sure that movement of the kick-starter pedal does not rotate the rear wheel, with the clutch engaged. On 1955 and later Nortons open the throttle very slightly by turning the twist-grip *inwards* about one-eighth of an inch (as measured at the rim of the twist-grip rubber).

If the engine is stone cold, close the air lever completely, and retard the ignition lever so that it is half-way between the full advance and full retard positions. This, of course, applies to magneto ignition models. On coil ignition models which have no ignition lever, turn the ignition key on top of the headlamp switch *clockwise* to IGN. Also momentarily depress the tickler on the float chamber, but do not flood the carburettor so that petrol begins to drip. If the engine has been previously warmed up, the air lever should be opened very slightly and the carburettor tickler should not be touched. It is assumed there is no backlash in the controls.

Difficult engine starting is often attributable to faulty control setting, and it is essential to *keep the throttle lever nearly closed* when endeavouring to start. Only thus can a high velocity air stream be induced over the pilot jet.

Starting Up. If the engine is unduly stiff in cold weather, free the piston before attempting to start up. The best method is to kick the engine over quickly about half a dozen times, with the exhaust-valve lifter fully raised.

To start, stand astride or beside the machine, put the piston on compression, raise the exhaust-valve lifter and depress the kick-starter a further 2–3 in. Release the exhaust-valve lifter and permit the kick-starter to return to its normal position. Then give a long swinging kick, carrying the starter round as far as possible. With the engine and carburettor in proper order, a start should be effected on the third kick at the most. Failure to start quickly is usually due to some definite defect such as plug trouble.

A prevalent source of difficult engine-starting is an over-rich mixture caused by excessive flooding of the carburettor or by numerous ineffectual attempts with the kick-starter, made worse perhaps by a low temperature. To clear the combustion chamber of vaporized fuel, open both the throttle twist-grip and air lever to their full extent and kick over the engine several times.

When the engine starts up, adjust the controls to give a sweet "pilot" tick-over. Advance the air lever fully, or nearly fully, and similarly advance the ignition lever (on Magdyno models). Do not "rev" up the engine *until the oil is circulating properly and has warmed up*. Sudden engine racing, especially when not under load, is most injurious. Never continue to run an engine in a closed garage, and do not allow a cold engine to run too slowly; this causes low-temperature condensation. If a dry-sump lubricated engine starts to issue clouds of blue smoke when starting up, ignore this phenomenon, as the surplus oil will quickly be returned to the tank by the pump. Black smoke denotes an over-rich mixture.

Check Oil Circulation After Starting Up. Remove the oil filler cap and observe the oil issuing from the return pipe. After the engine has run a few minutes (*see* page 34) the return is spasmodic.

To Engage First Gear. Disengage the clutch by squeezing the handlebar lever, and move the foot gear-change pedal *upwards* to its *full* extent. If you fail to engage first gear readily with the motor-cycle stationary, rock the machine gently to and fro while maintaining slight pressure on the foot gear-change pedal (Fig. 5). Continue doing this until you feel that first gear is engaged.

Moving Off. Open the throttle slightly by turning the throttle twist-grip *inwards*, and gently and progressively engage the clutch by releasing the handlebar lever. As the clutch engages and the motor-cycle gathers momentum, open the throttle a little more. Should any slight pinking on a magneto ignition model occur, immediately retard the ignition very slightly, or close the air lever a shade. For all normal running after the engine has warmed up, keep the ignition lever fully advanced and on all models the air lever wide open.

Change from First to Second Gear. Gear-changing is rapidly mastered, and gear crashing of a serious nature is impossible because all pinions are of the constant-mesh type. Speed up the machine to about 15 m.p.h., declutch, and simultaneously throttle down the engine, wait a second until mainshaft and layshaft are running at the same speed, and depress the foot change fully, afterwards letting in the clutch gently and throttling up to take the increased load. *Never employ force on the foot change.* All operations should be quick, but accurate and progressive, and *no attempt should ever be made to change gear without first declutching*, for in this case we have dog clutches being induced to mesh while being driven at different speeds. *On no account allow the engine to knock* (i.e. make a metallic noise) by driving it too slowly under load or in the case of a magneto model with too advanced ignition timing. A change to a lower gear should be made immediately the engine shows signs of distress, *but do not slip the clutch as an alternative to gear-changing.*

Change from Second to Third Gear. Proceed as before. Speed up the machine until it has plenty of momentum, declutch, throttle down, wait a second, and smartly move the foot change down fully until third gear is felt to engage; afterwards engage the clutch and throttle up again until the desired speed is reached.

Change from Third to Fourth Gear. To get into top gear, follow the previous procedure. Throttle up, declutch, ease off the throttle, wait momentarily and push the pedal down until fourth gear is felt to engage.

The tendency for knocking, if any, is during the change from third to fourth, and the controls should be handled judiciously to counteract this, especially if the change is made on an up-gradient, when the engine revolutions should be kept high during the changes.

Making Downward Gear Changes. Simultaneously open the throttle slightly, disengage the clutch, and with toe pressure *raise* the foot gear-change pedal upwards to its full extent. Then quickly and progressively re-engage the clutch.

When making a gear change, hold the foot gear-change pedal in position with the toe until the gear is *felt* to engage and the clutch has been re-engaged. Make all gear changes quietly and smoothly.

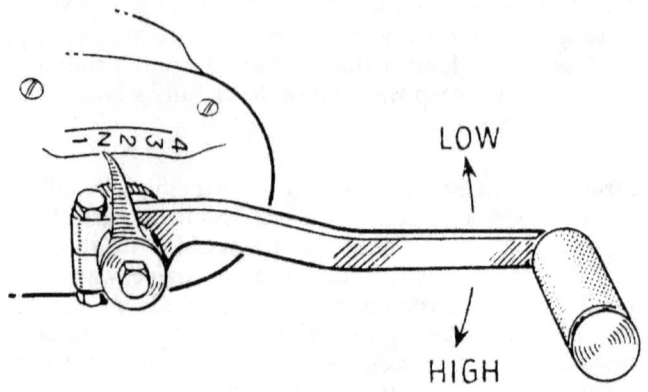

FIG. 5. THE FOOT GEAR-CHANGE PEDAL AND INDICATOR
The pedal automatically returns to the same position after each gear change.

Note that when changing down quickly from fourth or third gear into first gear it is not essential to disengage the clutch, to throttle up the engine, and to *re-engage the clutch* during each gear change. It is sufficient to slow down to a low speed, disengage the clutch, and make two or three full upward movements of the gear-change pedal in quick succession, according to whether third or fourth gear respectively was previously engaged. Each time you raise the gear-change pedal, "blip" the engine, i.e. throttle up slightly.

To Obtain "Neutral." It is necessary to change down into first gear, stop,* and then with the clutch still disengaged, *slightly* and very gently *depress* the foot gear-change pedal with the toe. In this instance do not move the pedal to its full extent, otherwise you will miss "neutral" and engage second gear. A "light touch" is required, and you should be careful to re-engage the clutch gradually in case a gear should have been accidentally engaged. Neutral lies between first and second gears (*see* Fig. 5).

* An expert can obtain neutral without first stopping the machine.

Running-in. After taking delivery of a brand new Norton, special care must be exercised for 1,000 miles when driving. *Until 500 miles have been covered, a speed in excess of 40 m.p.h. in top gear on the level should not be attained;* keep down to correspondingly lower maximum speeds in the other gears, and nurse a rebored engine carefully for 1,000 miles. Besides avoiding excessive speed, avoid opening the throttle more than one-quarter to one-third, and never allow the engine to labour by neglecting to make full use of the gearbox, otherwise it will never attain maximum efficiency, and its performance will probably be spoiled. Speed can be varied but the engine must always be run lightly loaded. Increase speed *progressively* as mileage increases.

Piston Seizure. Piston seizure is the only kind of seizure likely to arise through over-driving a new machine which has not been thoroughly run-in. If piston seizure (indicated by sudden loss of power and gradual slowing up) should occur, whip out the clutch and throttle down instantly. Allow the engine to cool before continuing, and at the first opportunity examine the cylinder barrel and piston for scoring. Slight scoring of the piston skirt can sometimes be overlooked, and the same applies to very slight score marks on the cylinder bore. But if the cylinder bore is marred by numerous and rather deep scores, it will be necessary to have the cylinder barrel rebored and an oversize piston and rings fitted. Pre-ignition, due to an unsuitable plug, produces symptoms rather similar to those of piston seizure.

Suitable Sparking Plugs. On all 1955 and later Models 19, ES2 and 50 requiring 14-mm. sparking plugs, suitable types to fit are the Lodge 2HLN, the K.L.G. FE75 or FE80, or the Champion N5. Prior to 1958 the Champion N5 was known as the NA-8, and this type is still suitable. Note that Champion plugs, unlike the Lodge and K.L.G. types, cannot be dismantled for cleaning.

CHAPTER II

LUCAS DYNAMO LIGHTING (1955–8 MODELS)

INSTRUCTIONS for the maintenance of the magneto unit of the Lucas "Magdyno" fitted to 1955–8 Models 19, ES2 and 50 are on page 55. This chapter deals with the dynamo portion alone, together with the lamps and battery. On 1959 and later coil ignition Models ES2 and 50 with Lucas alternator, rectifier, battery, coil, etc. the lighting and ignition equipment is combined and is therefore dealt with in a separate chapter.

DYNAMO MAINTENANCE

Before interfering with the wiring, always disconnect the battery positive lead (about one foot long)* from the switch lead, to avoid the danger of

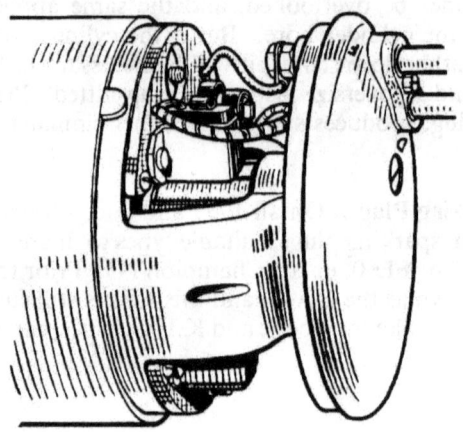

FIG. 6. COMMUTATOR END OF LUCAS E3LM DYNAMO
No lubricator is fitted.

short circuits which might cause serious damage. To disconnect, move the rubber shield and unscrew the cable connector; do not touch the frame with the connector and cause a short circuit. When reconnecting, pull the rubber shield well over the connector.

If at any time the motor-cycle must be ridden with the battery disconnected,

* On 1955 and later Nortons having a "pre-focus" type headlamp, a positive-earth system is used, and the battery *negative* lead should be disconnected.

or in any way out of service, it is essential to run with the switch in the *"OFF" position* (compensated-voltage-control excepted).

Inspection of Brushgear. It is advisable about every six months to remove the metal cover-band from the dynamo and inspect the brushgear and commutator. When removing the cover-band it is not necessary to disconnect either lead from the battery.

See that the dynamo brushes work freely in their holders. This can be easily ascertained by holding back each retaining spring and gently pulling each flexible lead; the brush should move without the slightest sluggishness. It should also return to its original position directly the lead is let go. When testing a brush in this way, release it gently, otherwise it may get chipped. The brushes should be clean and "bed" over the whole surface; that is, the face in contact with the commutator should appear uniformly polished. Dirty or sticking brushes may be cleaned, after removal, with a cloth moistened with petrol. Always replace carbon brushes in their original positions and see that they make firm contact with the commutator segments.

If the brushes become badly worn, remove them as follows. Release the eyelet on the brush lead by unscrewing the hexagonal nut or screw at the terminal. Then, holding back the spring lever out of the way, withdraw the brush from its holder. Replace with genuine Lucas brushes.

The brush springs should be inspected occasionally to see that they have sufficient tension to keep the brushes firmly pressed against the commutator when the machine is running; keep this in mind when the brushes have been in use a long time and are very much worn down. It is unwise to insert brushes of a grade other than that supplied with the dynamo, or to change the tension springs. When the brushes become so worn that they no longer bed down on the commutator, go to a Lucas service agent.

Commutator. The surface of the commutator should be kept clean and free from oil or brush dust, etc. Should any grease or oil work its way on to the commutator through over-lubrication, it will cause sparking and carbon and copper dust will be collected in the grooves between the commutator segments. The best way to clean the commutator without disconnecting any leads is to remove from its holder one of the two brushes and, inserting a dry cloth (moistened with petrol if the commutator is very dirty) in the holder, hold it, with a suitably-shaped piece of wood, against the commutator surface, causing the armature to be rotated at the same time. If the commutator has been neglected for a long period, it may need cleaning with fine glasspaper. The segments should be *dark bronze* and highly polished.

Terminals. On a Lucas "Magdyno" with a separate voltage-control unit the positive dynamo terminal is marked D and the shunt-field terminal *F* on the cover. To connect, first slacken the fixing screws on the terminal block and remove the clamping plate. Then withdraw the metal sleeve from each terminal. The cables should then be passed through the clamping plate holes and bared at the ends for ⅜ in. Now fit the sleeves over the cables, bend back the wires over them and push the sleeves home into the terminals, finally screwing down the clamping plate shown in Fig. 7.

Lucas Servicing. It is a good plan every 10,000 miles to entrust the dynamo to a Lucas service depot for dismantling, cleaning, servicing, and lubrication. The bearings will be repacked with grease.

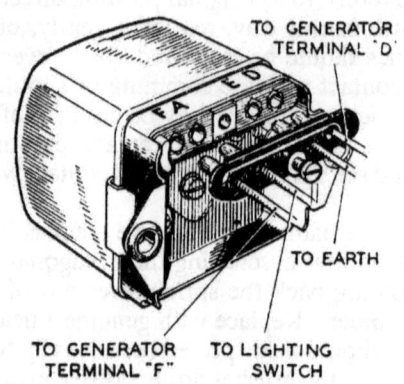

Fig. 7. Lucas Cut-out and Regulator Unit Showing the Connexions

Compensated Voltage Control. This is used on all 1955-8 Nortons. Wiring diagrams are given on pages 21–2. The control unit comprises the cut-out and voltage control (working on the trembler principle) neatly housed in a casing inside the tool box. The unit sees to it that the battery is kept properly charged automatically, the dynamo output varying according to the state of charge of the battery and the load.

With C.V.C. equipment the lighting switch is provided with only three positions—*Off*, *L*, and *H* (*see* page 18). In all three positions the dynamo gives a controlled output, thus relieving the rider of much responsibility. The regulator begins to operate when the dynamo voltage reaches about 7·3 volts. During daylight running when the battery is well charged the ammeter may indicate a charge of only 1 or 2 amp, for the dynamo gives only a trickle charge. The cut-out prevents the battery discharging when the dynamo is not charging.

The regulator provides for an increase of dynamo output as soon as the lamps are switched on. The effect of switching the lamps on after a long run with the battery voltage high is often to cause a temporary discharge reading at the ammeter, but fairly soon the voltage falls and the regulator responds, thereby causing the output of the dynamo to balance the load of the lamps.

When the battery is in a discharged state, the regulator increases the dynamo output and restores the battery to it normal state of charge in the shortest possible time.

Do Not Tamper with the C.V.C. Unit. The unit is sealed by the makers, and does not need adjustment once it is correctly set. The only conceivable trouble is from the contacts oxidizing or welding together, owing to accidental crossing of the dynamo field and positive leads. Be careful if making wiring alterations (*see* page 10). Referring to Fig. 7, make sure that the C.V.C. unit connexions are correct, tight, and that the insulation is sound.

Removing and Replacing Dynamo. On 1955 and later "Magdyno" models with compensated-voltage-control, first disconnect the connexions from the dynamo terminals. Unscrew the hexagon nut from the "Magdyno" driving-end cover. Then loosen the two screws which fasten the band clip. The dynamo can then be withdrawn from the rest of the "Magdyno" unit.

On assembling the dynamo, slide it through the band clip so that the fixing screw passes through the hole in the end cover. See that the gears mesh properly. Tighten the end-cover nut and the two band-clip securing screws. Then connect up the connexions to the dynamo terminals. Verify that this is correctly done. Referring to Fig. 7, it will be noted that the cable from the cut-out and regulator terminal *D* is connected to a similarly marked terminal on the dynamo. The same applies to the cut-out and regulator terminal marked *F*.

Absence of Fuses. In order to simplify the system as far as possible, no fuse is provided. If all the connexions are kept clean and tight, there is no possibility of any excess current causing damage to the equipment.

Ammeter. This indicates the amount of current flowing into or from the battery and shows whether the battery is being charged or discharged. It is of the centre-zero type and fitted on top of the headlamp.

CARE OF THE LUCAS BATTERY

The Lucas battery must receive regular attention to keep it in good condition.

The following are the most important maintenance hints—
1. Keep the electrolyte level with the tops of the separators.
2. Add only distilled water, never tap water.
3. Test the condition of the battery by taking occasional readings of the specific gravity of the acid with a hydrometer.
4. Never leave the battery in a discharged condition.

Top-up the Cells Regularly. Examine the acid level about once a fortnight, and even more frequently in tropical climates. Unscrew and remove the battery clamping screw and washer securing the metal strap (some 1955 models). On later models the battery is held inside the front compartment of the tool box by a "U" bolt pointing upwards at an angle from the bottom inside corner of the tool-box compartment, and a clamping strap bears on the corner of the battery which has no lid; release the strap. Take off the battery lid (1955 models) and remove the three vent plugs. Inspect the hole in each vent plug and make certain that it is not obstructed. A choked vent plug hole will result in an increase of pressure in the cell owing to "gassing," and this may cause trouble. Remove any dirt with a bent wire.

Wipe the top of the battery clean with a rag and verify that the rubber washer, fitted beneath each vent plug to prevent leakage, is in position. Make sure that the rubber washer fitted under each vent plug is undamaged After wiping the top of the battery, destroy the rag. See that a supply of clean distilled water is to hand.

Be careful not to hold a naked light near the vents. If the level is below the tops of the separators, add *distilled* water* as required with a Lucas battery filler (*see* Fig. 9) to bring the level correct. This should be done just *before* a charge run, as the agitation due to running and the gassing will thoroughly mix the solution. Insert the nozzle of the battery filler into each cell until the nozzle rests on the separators. Hold the filler in this position until air bubbles stop rising in the glass container. The cell is then topped-up to the correct level.

Acid must not be added to the electrolyte unless the solution has been spilled. If the solution has been spilled by accident, add diluted sulphuric acid of specific gravity equal to that in the cells.

Replenishing the Lucas Battery Filler. When replenishing the Lucas battery filler with distilled water, see that the screw-on nozzle is replaced correctly. The rubber washer must be fitted over the valve with the small peg in the centre of the valve engaging the hole in the projecting boss of the washer.

Checking Specific Gravity. Occasionally, hydrometer readings (specific gravity values) should be taken of the solution in each of the cells. The method of doing this is shown in Fig. 10. The Lucas hydrometer contains a graduated float which indicates the specific gravity of the electrolyte in the battery cell from which a sample is taken.

After a sample has been taken and checked, it must, of course, be returned to the cell. The taking of S.G. readings with a hydrometer is the most efficient way of ascertaining the state of charge of the battery. The

* The distilled water, unlike the sulphuric acid, is lost gradually by evaporation.

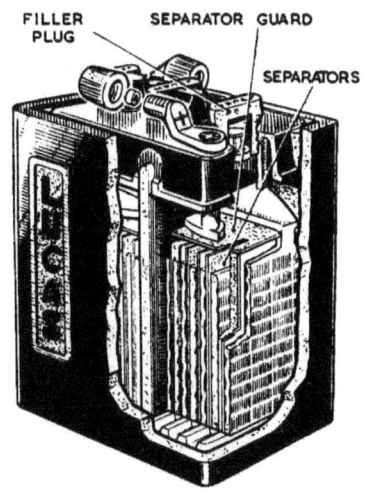

Fig. 8. The Lucas PU7E/II Type Battery
The battery is housed with the C.V.C. unit inside the tool box.

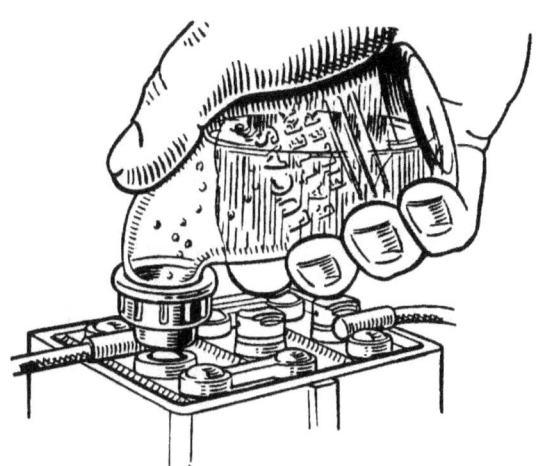

Fig. 9. Topping-up the Cells with a Lucas Battery Filler

Most Lucas batteries fitted to Models 19, ES2 and 50 have an acid-level device resting on a ledge below each vent plug orifice. To top-up, pour distilled water round each perforated flange until no more drains into the battery cell. Lift the tube slightly to clear the water from the flange and the level is correct.

S.G. readings should be approximately the *same for all three cells*. Should the reading for one cell differ substantially from the readings for the others, probably some acid has been spilled, or has leaked from the cell concerned. There is also a possibility of a short-circuit between the battery plates. If so, return the battery to a Lucas service depot for attention.

The battery must never be permitted to remain in a discharged condition for long, or serious deterioration will occur. After checking the S.G.

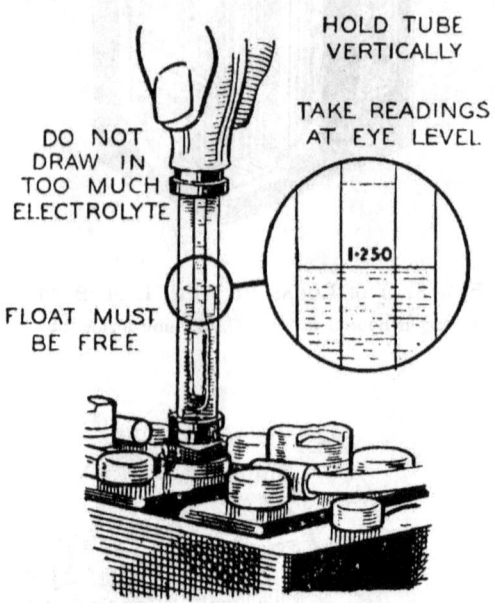

FIG. 10. LUCAS HYDROMETER BEING USED TO CHECK SPECIFIC GRAVITY OF ELECTROLYTE

readings and topping-up the cells, wipe the top of the battery and remove any spilled electrolyte or water; replace the three vent plugs and the battery lid (1955). Then position and tighten the battery strap.

Battery Connexions. Always keep the connexions clean, free from corrosion, and tight, otherwise the ammeter readings will *not* indicate the true state of charge of the battery. To prevent corrosion, smear screw-type connexions with petroleum jelly. If disconnecting the battery, note which terminal is connected to the machine and reconnect accordingly.

Correct Readings. With Lucas batteries fitted to Nortons, the specific gravity readings at an acid temperature of approximately 60°F should be: 1·280–1·300, battery fully charged; about 1·200 battery about half discharged; below 1·150, battery fully discharged.

A low state of charge is often caused through parking the machine for long periods with the lighting switch in the *L* position, unaccompanied by much daylight running. The remedy is, of course, to undertake more daylight running and to keep the switch in the *Off* position as much as possible until the battery regains its normal state of charge. If overcharging occurs, have the setting of the compensated-voltage-control unit checked.

Concerning Cables (1957–8). To connect cables to the Lucas battery, unscrew the knurled plastic nut and withdraw the collet. Bare about one inch of cable and thread through the knurled nut and collet. Next bend the cable strands back over the small end of the collet. Draw back into the nut and tighten the nut on the terminal.

Snap connectors (rubber covered push-pull connexions) are employed widely throughout the lighting circuit, and appear when connected as a small rubber sleeve or bunch of sleeves when grouped. Disconnect by pulling apart and reconnect by holding in the pliers the metal nipple soldered to the cable end. Hold the rubber covered portion in the fingers and press home the cable with pliers. Make sure that the rubber sleeves are always covering the metal portion of the connectors when in use.

Storage. If the equipment is laid by for several months, the battery must be given a full charge and afterwards given a refreshing charge from a separate source of electrical energy about once a fortnight, to obviate any permanent sulphation of the plates. In no circumstances must the electrolyte be removed from the battery and the plates allowed to dry, or permanent loss of capacity will result.

THE LUCAS LAMPS

Several different types of Lucas headlamps and tail lamps have been fitted to 1955 and later Nortons.

SSU700P1 Headlamps (1955). To render the bulbs accessible, first remove the lamp front with Lucas light-unit assembly. Slacken the securing screw at the top of the lamp and then detach the front rim, complete with light-unit assembly. When replacing, locate the bottom of the light-unit assembly in the lamp body, press on the front, and secure in position by tightening the securing screw.

The "pre-focus" Lucas SSU700P/1 headlamp with underslung pilot light (Fig. 11) used on some 1955 Norton models has *no focusing adjustment*, and the main bulb cannot be inserted incorrectly (*see* page 20). The pilot bulb is carried in a detachable plate.

MCH58 and MCH61 Headlamps (1956–8). The speedometer, lighting switch, and ammeter are mounted on a panel secured by three set-screws to the top of the MCH58 headlamp fitted to 1956 Nortons. All 1957–8 models have the MCH61 headlamp which has a one-piece shell with no panel. The wiring harness enters through the rear of the lamp body, and is clamped to prevent chafing. The headlamp has a Lucas F700 light-unit assembly which includes a block-type lens and an aluminized reflector, proof against tarnishing.

A plug-in type pilot light (recommended for parking only) is located inside the reflector below the double-filament "pre-focus" main bulb. To gain access to both bulbs, remove the lamp front with sealed-beam light

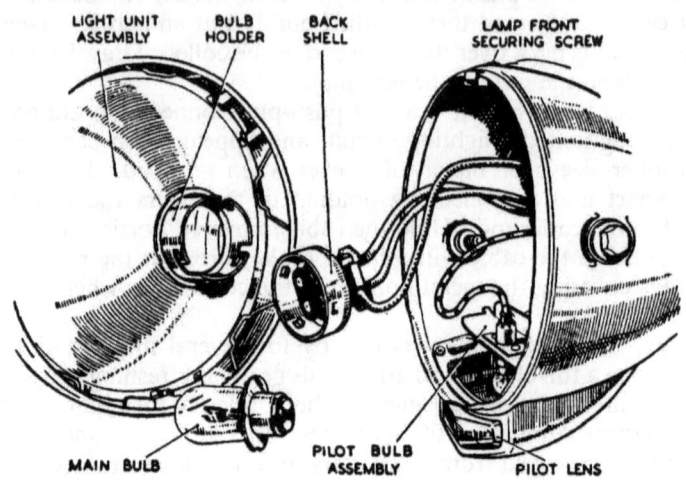

Fig. 11. Lucas SSU700P/1 "Pre-focus" Headlamp with Light-unit Assembly (and Main Bulb) Removed (1955 Models with Underslung Pilot Light)

unit assembly, after slackening the securing screw at the top of the lamp. When replacing, locate the bottom of the light-unit assembly in the lamp body, press on the front, and secure by tightening the fixing screw at the top of the lamp.

The "pre-focus" main bulb is of similar type (*see* Fig. 11) as that used with the SSU700P/1 headlamp. It cannot be fitted incorrectly, neither can it be focused.

Switch Positions (1955–8). Compensated-voltage-control is provided on all 1955 and later models, and therefore the dynamo charges the battery when the engine is running with the lighting switch in *any* of its three positions which are as follows—

Off: Headlamp, tail lamp, and sidecar lamp (when fitted) switched off.

L: Headlamp pilot bulb, tail lamp, speedometer, and sidecar lamp (where fitted) on.

H: Headlamp main bulb, tail lamp, speedometer, and sidecar lamp (where fitted) on.

Adjusting the Headlamp Position. If the headlamp is incorrectly aligned maximum road illumination will not be obtained, and other road users may be inconvenienced by dazzle. It is easy to rectify this fault.

The best method of checking the alignment of the headlamp is to stand your Norton facing a light-coloured wall at a distance of about 25 feet.

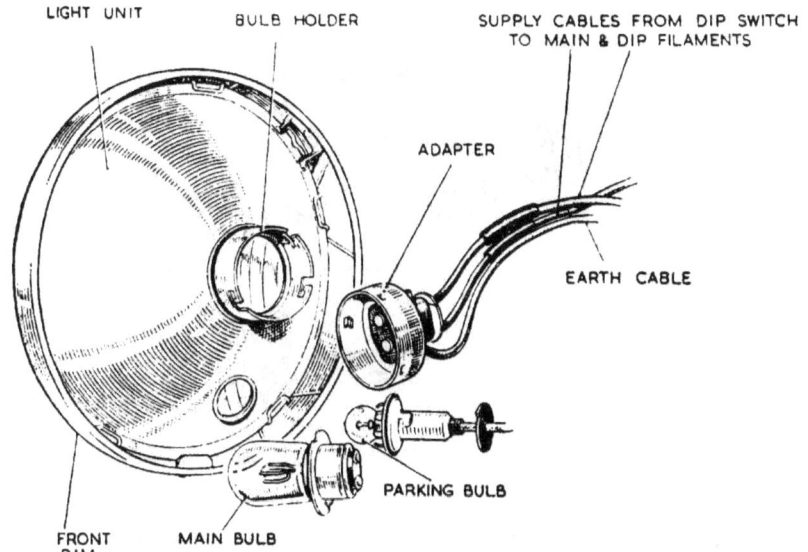

FIG. 12. LIGHT-UNIT, MAIN BULB AND PILOT BULB REMOVED FROM "PRE-FOCUS" HEADLAMP (1956–8 MODELS 19, ES2, 50)

Switch on the main driving light and note if the beam is projected straight ahead and parallel with the ground (which should be level).

Take vertical measurements from the centre of the headlamp, and from the centre of the illuminated circle on the wall, to the ground. Both measurements should be equal. If not, loosen the two fixing bolts securing the headlamp in the front fork mounting brackets and tilt the headlamp until the centre of the beam is truly parallel with the ground. Afterwards tighten the two fixing bolts firmly.

Stop-tail Lamp (1953 Onwards). A very good design of stop-tail lamp (Model 525) is fitted to 1955 and later machines, and a reflex red reflector is also included. To remove the moulded red plastic cover, it is only necessary to remove two captive screws (*see* Fig. 13). This gives access to the double-filament bulb. One 6-watt filament is provided for the normal rear light and number plate illumination, and an 18-watt filament for the stop light to indicate when the motor-cycle is braking. The bulb holder has staggered slots to ensure the correct fitting of the bulb.

Cleaning Lucas Lamps. Clean the lamp body with a good car polish, and polish the chromium-plated rim with a chamois leather or a soft, dry duster. First wash off all dirt with water. On no account use metal polish

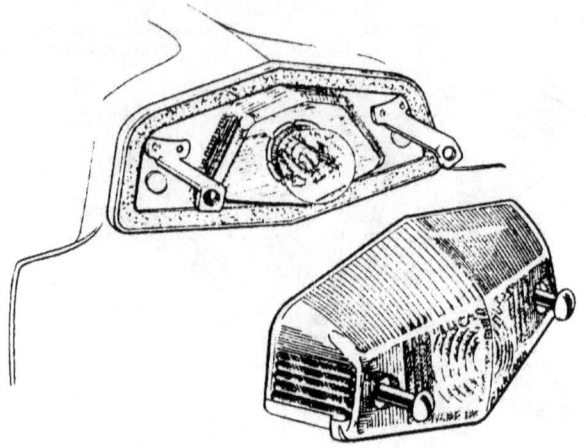

FIG. 13. THE LUCAS 525 STOP-TAIL LAMP (1955-8)

to clean the reflector. Keep the glass of the light-unit clean. To remove finger marks, polish the reflector with a chamois leather or with a *very* soft dry cloth.

BULB RENEWAL

SSU700P/1 Headlamp Bulb Replacements (1955). Where a Lucas type SSU700P/1 headlamp with "pre-focus" bulb (*see* Fig. 11) is fitted, the correct bulb replacements are—

Main bulb—6-volt, 30/30 watt, double-filament Lucas No. 312.

Pilot bulb—6-volt, 3 watt, Lucas No. 988.

All 1955 SSU700P/1 headlamps are of the "pre-focus" type (*see* Fig. 11) with no focusing adjustment, and they require a No. 312 6-volt, 30/24 watt main bulb which can be fitted in one position only.

The No. 312 "pre-focus" bulb is easy to identify as it has a broad locating flange on its cap. It cannot be fitted incorrectly.

Referring to Fig. 11, to replace a No. 312 "pre-focus" main bulb, first slacken the screw at the top of the headlamp and lift off the front rim complete with light unit assembly. Then turn the back shell of the "pre-focus" bulb *anti-clockwise*, pull it off, and remove the bulb from the rear of

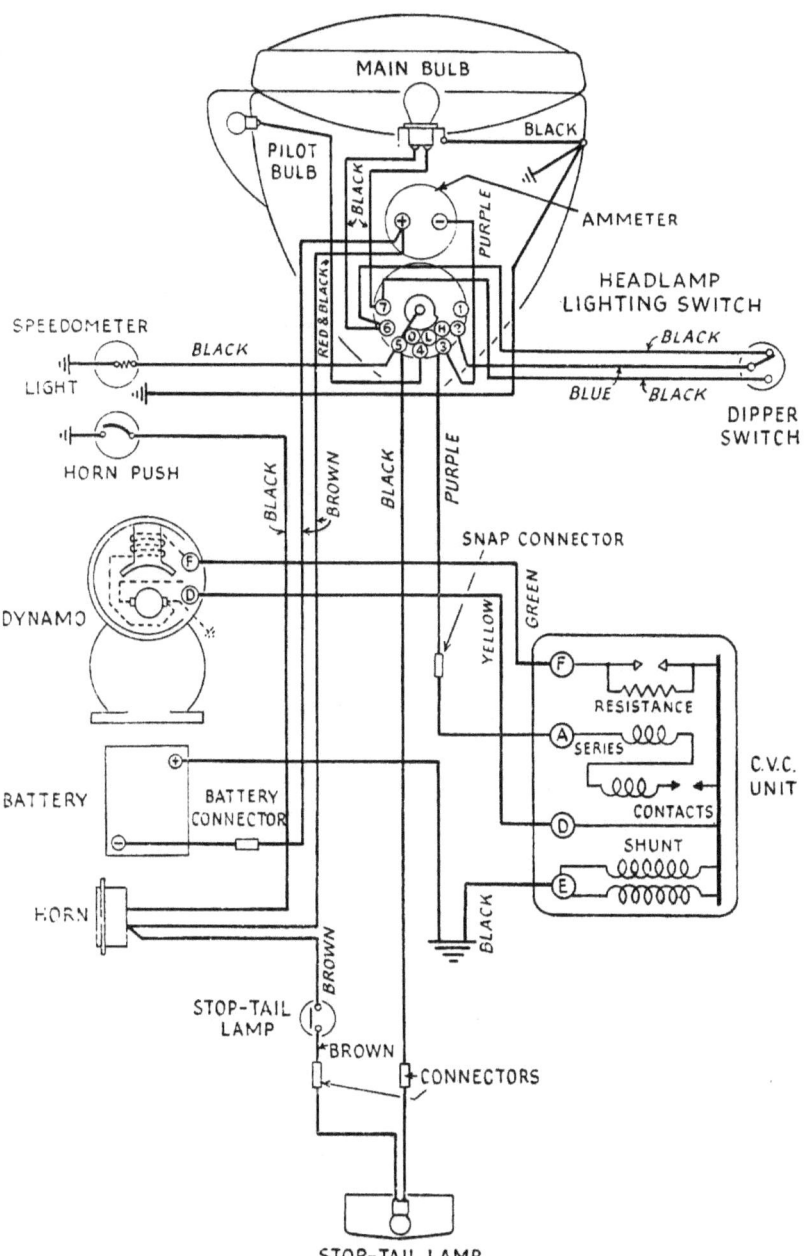

FIG. 14. WIRING DIAGRAM FOR LUCAS "MAGDYNO" LIGHTING EQUIPMENT WITH SSU700P/1 HEADLAMP

This applies to all the 1955 Nortons with compensated-voltage-control and a "positive earth" system of wiring. On 1955 models the lead to the stop-tail lamp is taken from the battery negative instead of from the horn as shown. The battery positive lead has *black* sleeving.

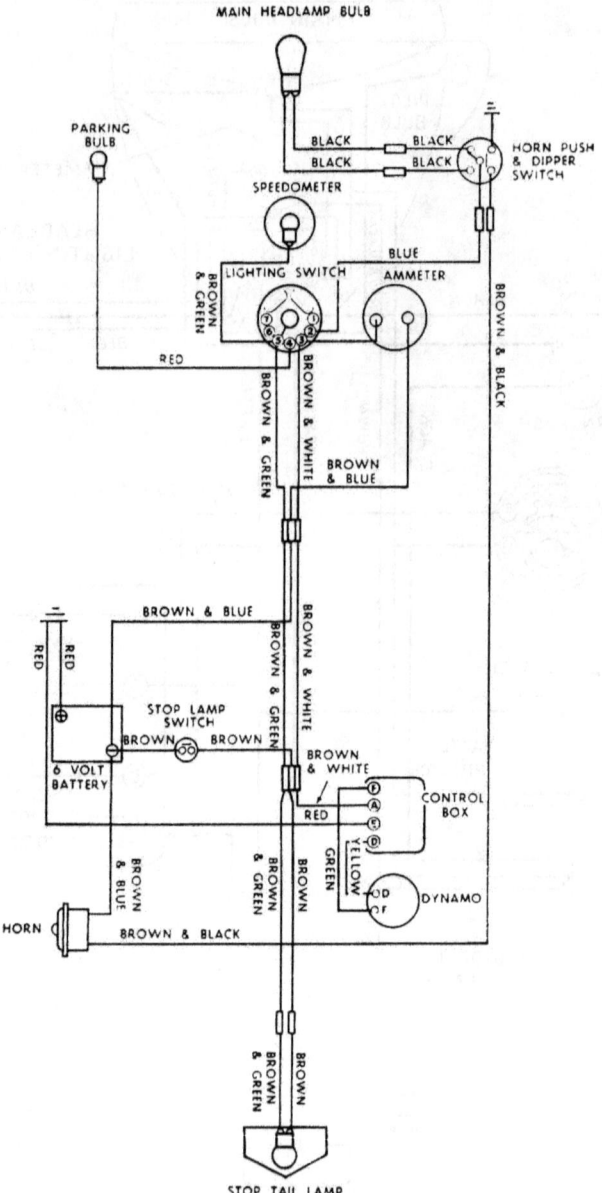

FIG. 14A. WIRING DIAGRAM FOR LUCAS "MAGDYNO" LIGHTING EQUIPMENT WITH MCH58 HEADLAMP
This applies to the 1956-8 Models 19, ES2, 50.

the reflector. Fit the new bulb (No. 312) in the holder, engage the projections on the inside of the back shell with the slots in the bulb holder, press on the shell, and secure by turning clockwise.

If the pilot bulb of a "pre-focus" SSU700P/1 Lucas headlamp requires renewal, slide out the metal plate above the underslung pilot lens, and fit to it a 6-volt, 3 watt, Lucas No. 988 bulb. See that the metal plate is pressed firmly home afterwards, or it may work free while riding and cause the pilot light to go out, possibly unobserved by the rider.

Headlamp Bulb Replacements (1956-62). Where a Lucas type MCH58 or MCH61 headlamp with "pre-focus" main bulb (*see* Fig. 12) is fitted, the correct bulb replacements are—
Main bulb—6-volt, 30/24 watt, double-filament Lucas No, 312 or 373.*
Pilot bulb—6-volt, 3 watt, Lucas No. 988.
Referring to Fig. 12, to replace a No. 373 "pre-focus" main bulb, first slacken the screw at the top of the headlamp and lift off the front rim complete with light-unit assembly. Then remove and replace the No. 373 main bulb exactly as described previously for the SSU700P/1 headlamp.

The pilot bulb is a spring fit in the rear of the reflector. When withdrawing the holder be careful not to lose the rubber washer.

Stop-tail Lamp (1955-59). The correct bulb for a Lucas "525" stop-tail lamp is a Lucas No. 384 6-volt, 6/18 watt double-filament type. See that the bulb is secure in the slotted holder before securing the plastic cover with the two screws. (*See* also page 24.)

* The No. 312 bulb gives a vertical dip, but No. 373 dips to the left.

CHAPTER III

THE LIGHTING AND IGNITION SYSTEM (1959-62 MODELS)

THE 1959-62 Models ES2 and 50 have coil instead of magneto ignition and on these models the lighting and ignition equipment are not independent as is the case where a dynamo is fitted.

The 1959-62 equipment comprises the Lucas headlamp (*see* page 21), a combined lighting and ignition switch, a Lucas alternator, a Lucas or Exide battery, a rectifier, a coil, and a contact-breaker.

The Lighting and Ignition Switch. The lighting switch positions are referred to on page 18 and the ignition key in the centre of the lighting switch on page 3. The switch is complicated, and do not attempt to dismantle it for any reason. The switch connexions are accessible when the headlamp front and light unit assembly is removed.

Under normal running conditions (with the ignition key in the IGN position, rectified alternating current passes to the battery from the alternator. The rate of output depends on the lighting switch position. With front and rear lights out the alternator output supplies the ignition coil and trickle-charges the battery. When the lighting switch is turned on the alternator output is automatically increased.

The Lucas Headlamp. For details of removing the bulbs for replacement, *see* page 21). The correct bulbs to fit in the Lucas MCH61 headlamp are stated on page 21. Always keep the headlamp position adjusted as dealt with on page 19). If you carry a pillion passenger for night riding, set the beam so that with two persons on the machine the beam is horizontal or slightly below.

The Dipper Switch. Sticking of the switch prevents instantaneous changeover from one headlamp filament to the other and can be very dangerous. It is desirable to connect the dipper switch so that the dipped beam is in use when the switch lever is lowered. Oil the dipper switch pivot and toggle lever occasionally.

The Stop-tail Lamp. The Lucas "564" stop-tail lamp shown in Fig. 15 is fitted to 1960 and later models, but on the 1959 models the "525" lamp shown in Fig. 13 is fitted. The "564" lamp has twin "Reflex" reflectors and requires a double-filament bulb having a 6-watt filament for the normal rear and number plate light and an 18-watt filament controlled by the rear brake.

LIGHTING AND IGNITION SYSTEM

To obtain access to the double-filament bulb, remove the two securing screws and the plastic lens complete. The bulb has unequally positioned bayonet pins, so that it cannot be fitted incorrectly into the holder.

Emergency Starting. As stated on page 3, an emergency starting position is provided for the ignition key for use if the battery is discharged. With the key moved to the EMG position, the alternator is connected direct to the ignition coil. This permits the engine to be started independently of the battery. After starting turn the ignition key to IGN.

Note that when using the kick-starter with the ignition key in the EMG position, considerably more force may be necessary than is required for a normal start. Should the ignition timing for any reason be only slightly different than the correct timing, an EMG start may prove impossible. In this case try a push start with the ignition key in the normal IGN position and the machine in second gear.

Should the alternator leads have been changed over (*see* page 26) to obtain an increased charge rate, it may be found impossible to start up with the ignition key in the EMG position. Here the leads should be temporarily changed back or a push start attempted.

The Lucas Alternator. Because the Lucas alternator (types RM15 and RM19) has no commutator, brush mechanism, bearings, or oil seals the only maintenance required is occasionally to check that its leads are intact and its connectors clean and tight. Inspect the grummet in the rear half of the oil-bath chaincase because if this is perished the leads may chafe on the relatively sharp edge of the hole. Note that there should always be at least 0·005 in. clearance between the rotor and the pole pieces on the stator. Check this clearance whenever occasion is had to refit the stator. Observe that the stator should be fitted with the lead take-off side towards the primary chain and *not* towards the outer portion of the oil-bath chaincase.

To remove the rotor which has a key remove the nut securing it. If the rotor is tight on the shaft and the shaft is parallel it may be necessary to remove the stator which is secured on most models by three nuts and fan disc washers.

When the rotor is removed it is quite unnecessary to fit keepers to the rotor poles. Wipe off any metal swarf which may have collected on the pole tips and place the rotor in a clean place.

The stator is capable of being fitted either way round into the spigot recess, but it will only operate satisfactorily in one position. It is fitted correctly when the edge from which the leads emerge is innermost or away from the oil-bath chaincase outer portion.

Increased Charging Rate. If the battery becomes badly discharged through extensive slow riding in traffic or during running-in, or because of parking with lights on for lengthy periods, and whenever a sidecar is

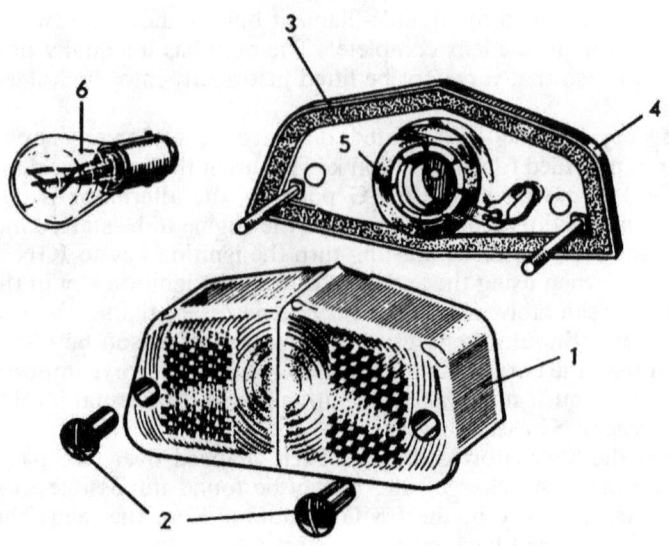

Fig. 15. The Lucas 564 Stop-tail Lamp (1960 Onwards)

1. Lens and window
2. Nut
3. Gasket
4. Base assembly
5. Grummet
6. Bulb

fitted, an increased charging rate can be effected through a simple alteration to the wiring.

The leads from the alternator after emerging from the oil-bath chaincase join the main harness by means of a three-way snap connector. On 1960–62 Models ES2 and 50 it may be necessary to remove the battery and

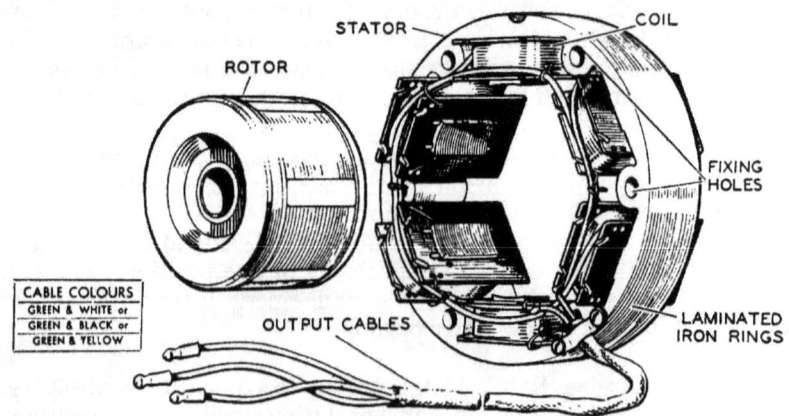

Fig. 16. The Lucas Alternator

LIGHTING AND IGNITION SYSTEM 27

battery box to gain access to the connector. The lead colours are: light green or green and white; dark green or green and black and green and yellow. Disconnect the dark green or green and black and the green and yellow and reverse these two connectors. Connect the green and black alternator cable to the green and yellow harness cable. Connect the green and black harness cable to the green and yellow alternator cable.

On some models (1959) there is a group of three rubber-covered snap connectors. Disconnect the green and yellow and dark green connectors and reconnect the dark green alternator cable to the green with yellow harness cable, and the green with yellow alternator cable to the dark green harness cable. Do not interfere with the light green cable.

With the lighting switch in the OFF position the ammeter should show approximately twice the previous output. When the lights are switched on to either "pilot" or "head," however, the output remains as previously.

Whenever a sidecar is permanently attached it is desirable to make this lead alteration, otherwise the current consumption of the sidecar lamp or lamps will not be compensated for and the battery will slowly discharge. When riding on a solo machine for a long distance in daylight, using the increased output, the battery may become overcharged and this may damage the battery and also the plated and enamelled parts of the motor-cycle through acid spillage.

The Rectifier. This device beneath the tool tray on most models converts A.C. to D.C. current and allows the current to flow in one direction only. This unit should require no attention whatever other than occasionally checking that the connexions are clean and tight. Pay special attention to the earth lead terminal connexion and the tension in the central bolt. Under no circumstances allow the nuts clamping the rectifier plates together to become slack. The pressure is carefully set during manufacture to give correct rectifier performance.

A separate nut is provided to attach the selenium type rectifier to the frame of the motor-cycle and it is most important periodically to check that the rectifier is firmly attached to its mounting point. To ensure a good electrical connexion, it should make firm metal to metal contact.

The Coil. A fluid-cooled coil of orthodox type is attached to a suitable position on the frame (usually the frame top tube) of the motor-cycle by a bolt and clip. As in the case of the rectifier, the coil should only require occasional checking for the tightness and cleanliness of its mounting and terminals.

Battery Maintenance. Detailed instructions on the proper maintenance of Lucas batteries are given on pages 13–17 and an illustration of the Lucas type PU7E/11 battery fitted to all 1959–62 Nortons is shown in Fig. 8. Examine the acid level after the machine has been standing and not immediately after a run when the electrolyte will be gassing and show a higher level (i.e., above the top of the separators). Should you fit an Exide battery, the level should be to, but not above, the lower of the two lines marked on the battery case. On all batteries the *positive* terminal must be earthed. General maintenance is the same as for the Lucas battery.

On Lucas batteries clean up the end of a terminal with a smooth file if you have any doubt about the screw on the terminal making firm contact. An Exide battery has a tag terminal secured with a screw and this must make clean contact with the terminal post of the battery.

Concerning Stop-tail Lamp Wiring. Keep all terminals and connexions tight, and be quite sure that the cables are clear of moving parts. Carefully examine the stop and tail lamp leads and see that they are properly positioned in the aluminium clip on the left-hand side number plate mounting stud. The clip must hold the connectors themselves, and the longer lead which passes round the inside of the mudguard must also be in the clips and not foul the tyre at the front end of the guard where it passes through the grummet. Feed back any surplus wire on the lamp side of the snap connectors through the grummet into the space between the number plate and outside of the mudguard.

The above remarks about stop-tail lamp leads apply to all standard type Nortons.

The Contact-breaker Gap. It is advisable to check the contact-breaker gap after running 500 miles on a new machine, and subsequently about every 6,000 miles. Checking the gap is quite simple. First remove the sparking plug and contact-breaker cover. Then rotate the engine until the contact points are wide open and insert a suitable feeler gauge between the points. The feeler gauge should be a sliding fit and the correct gap is 0·014 in. to 0·016 in.

To adjust the contact-breaker gap, keep the engine in the position which gives maximum contact opening and slacken the screw which secures the fixed contact plate (*see* Fig. 17). Now insert a screwdriver between the two studs on the base plate and the notch in the fixed plate, and adjust the position of the plate until the correct contact-breaker gap is obtained. Finally tighten the securing screw and re-check the gap.

Contact-breaker Maintenance. Besides keeping the contact-breaker gap correct, maintenance entails some lubrication and cleaning. This should be done about every 6,000 miles. Remove and clean the contact-breaker cover. Referring to Fig. 17, unscrew the two screws securing the contact-breaker base plate. Remove this plate and with some clean engine oil lubricate the automatic-advance mechanism, paying special attention to the pivots. Then refit the base plate.

LIGHTING AND IGNITION SYSTEM

Inspect the contact-breaker points and see that they are free from grease or oil. Clean the points with a fine carborundum stone or fine emery cloth should the points be found to be burned or discoloured. Wipe away all traces of dirt and dust with a petrol-moistened cloth. Note that cleaning of

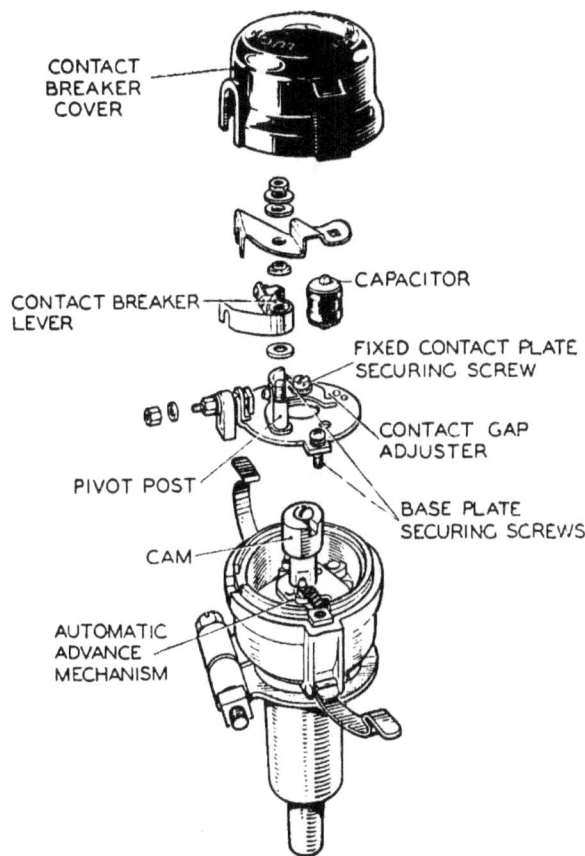

FIG. 17. THE CONTACT-BREAKER UNIT SHOWN DISMANTLED

The operating cam and the automatic-advance mechanism are also shown. All 1959–62 units are as shown. *See also* Fig. 43.

the contacts is facilitated if the lever which carries the moving contact is removed. Before replacing the contact-breaker lever, lightly smear the cam and pivot post with some oil.

The Chain Drive. The contact-breaker unit is chain driven from the inlet cam spindle. The sprocket is fitted on a taper and secured with a

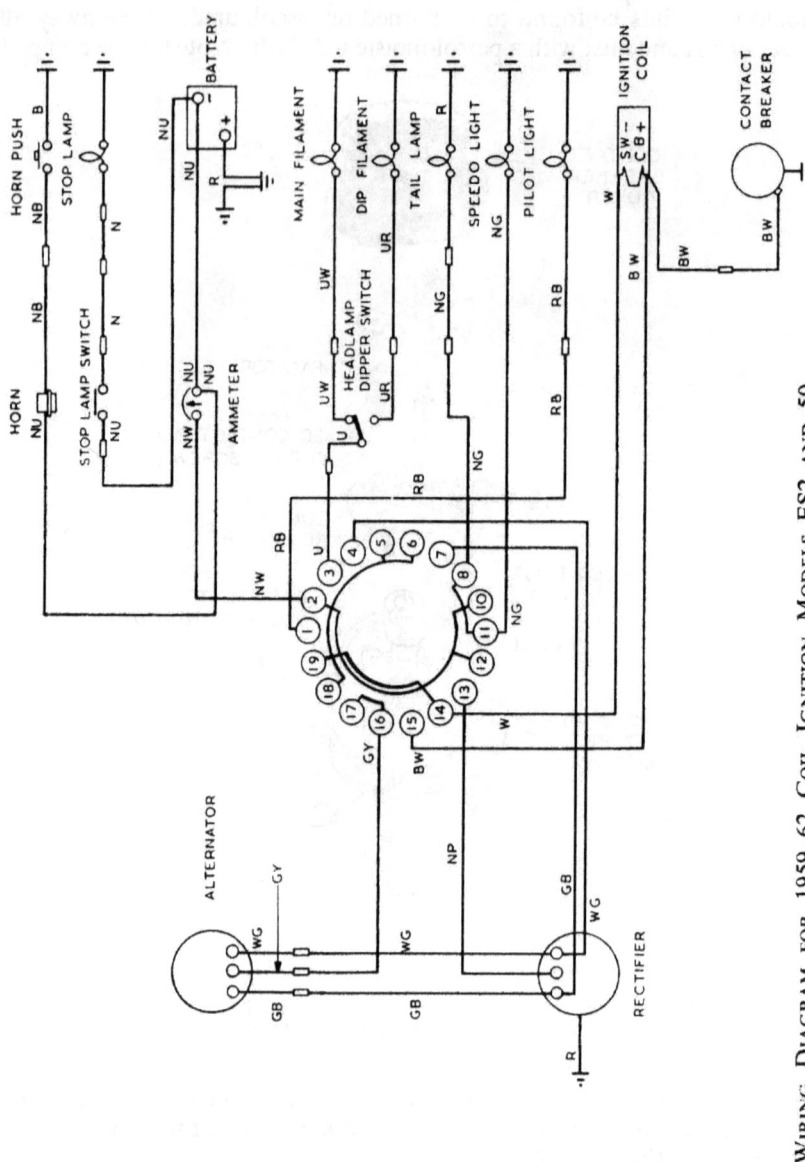

Fig. 18. Wiring Diagram for 1959–62 Coil Ignition Models ES2 and 50

LIGHTING AND IGNITION SYSTEM

central screw and washer. About every 2,000 miles remove the small screw in the top of the housing carrying the contact-breaker and into the oilway exposed, inject a few drops of engine oil.

Removal of Contact-breaker Unit. Normal routine maintenance does not necessitate the removal of the contact-breaker unit, but should this become necessary for some reason, proceed as follows. Remove the sprocket and single screw holding the clamping flange to the housing. Disconnect the coil wire from the terminal on the base plate. Then withdraw the contact-breaker unit.

The High Tension Cable. The condition of this cable is obviously most important. Renew a cable if it shows signs of cracking or perishing. Use 7 mm p.v.c. or Neoprene-covered vulcanized-rubber insulated ignition cable.

The Electric Horn. *See* notes below.

THE LIGHTING SWITCH AND HORN (1955-62)

The lighting switch and horn seldom develop trouble and are best left well alone. Should trouble occur somewhere in the wiring circuit, the accompanying wiring diagrams may prove useful, but those who have little electrical knowledge and do not possess a suitable voltmeter are advised to call at a Lucas service depot when any obscure fault in the wiring occurs.

The Switch. All electrical leads to the Lucas headlamp are taken direct to the lighting switch. On the SSU700P/1, and MCH58 Lucas headlamps referred to on pages 17-18 the switch, ammeter, and speedometer are mounted on a panel screwed to the headlamp shell.

Before attempting to remove the panel, it is wise to disconnect the appropriate battery lead (*see* page 10). To withdraw the panel from the headlamp it is only necessary to unscrew the three fixing screws. Note that the ends of all cables can be identified by means of coloured sleevings.

The Horn. This should give prolonged service without any attention because it is very carefully adjusted by the makers, and is not subjected to severe stresses. Do not assume that the horn has failed merely because its functioning becomes irregular, or because the horn ceases to vibrate. It is possible that a short-circuit has occurred in the wiring of the horn, a connexion is loose, or the battery is run down. Poor performance can also be caused by a slack horn fixing-bolt, or even by the vibration of some part close to the horn. In this case, hold the horn firmly in the hand by its bracket, and test for note. If unsatisfactory, get the horn examined and adjusted at a Lucas service depot.

CHAPTER IV

LUBRICATION

LUBRICATION, which consists of maintaining a microscopically thin film of oil on all contacting surfaces, can conveniently be divided into two groups: (a) engine lubrication; (b) cycle lubrication. On taking over a *new* machine it is only necessary to replenish the oil tank, other lubrication points having been attended to by the makers.

ENGINE LUBRICATION (1955-62)

There are three main parts in the engine where lubrication is vital: (a) at that part of the cylinder bore traversed by the piston and the piston rings (which reciprocate at exceptionally high speed); (b) the crankshaft assembly, including the two mainshaft bearings, and the big-end and small-end connecting-rod bearings; (c) the timing gear and the valve-operating gear.

The Dry-Sump Lubrication System (1955 Onwards). The D.S. lubrication system varies little on 1955 to 1962 Nortons. A gear-type pump similar to that illustrated in Fig. 19 is employed to force oil to: (a) the cylinder rear wall; (b) the double-row roller big-end bearing, and (c) the oil-pressure control valve. The return side of the pump picks up surplus oil and returns it to the tank. The gears on this side of the pump are twice as wide as those on the feed side, and therefore, having twice the pumping capacity, keep the crankcase "dry" when the engine is working.

With regard to cylinder lubrication, engine oil supplied by gravity from the tank (assisted by suction from the feed side of the oil pump) is pressure-fed by the delivery side of the oil pump to the crankcase mouth via the timing-case cover ducts, along the cylinder base, and then upwards through duct in the wall of the cylinder to the rear of the cylinder bore and the piston.

The big-end roller bearing is lubricated by oil pressure-fed through a timing-case cover duct, through the big-end restriction jet, through the timing-side main shaft, and then up a duct in the off-side flywheel to the roller big-end bearing itself.

The oil-pressure control valve functions as a safety valve in the oil circulation system. It has a spring-loaded ball which rises off its seat automatically as soon as the oil pressure reaches a predetermined value. Oil passing the valve becomes sprayed on the timing gears.

LUBRICATION

Surplus oil from the cylinder drains down the crankcase walls and is conveyed by ducts to the main-shaft bearings, and also to the bearings of the timing gears. The oil pump driving-pinion becomes immersed in oil because of the level of oil accumulated in the timing case. Consequently rotation of the pinion passes oil to the half-tine pinion and the timing gears.

On the O.H.V. Models 19, ES2, 50 a by-pass pipe leads from the oil *return* pipe to a banjo union on the rocker-box. Oil is thus fed to the rocker shafts and the ball ends of the overhead rockers. All surplus oil drains down to the crankcase through the two push-rod cover tubes. Surplus from the compartments housing the valve springs drains to the crankcase through holes drilled in the cylinder head and barrel.

FIG. 19. THE OIL PUMP (1955 ONWARDS) WITH BOTH PAIRS OF GEARS REMOVED

The contact-breaker chain on 1959–62 coil ignition models is lubricated by oil fed through the inlet cam spindle bush into the chaincase. Any excess oil in the case drains through the breather pipe.

The "Magdyno" chain on 1955–8 models is lubricated by oil passing through the inlet camshaft bush into the "Magdyno" chain case. Surplus oil accumulating in the case drains via the breather pipe. A timed breather is incorporated in the driving-side main-shaft and releases crankcase pressure through a small hole in the underside of the main-shaft bearing boss. Crankcase pressure is also released by a valve on the driving side of the crankcase and oil mist is fed to the secondary chain.

Surplus oil throughout the engine drains down to the crankcase base and enters a sludge trap (sludge comes away on removing the drain plug). The oil is then sucked up by the return side of the oil pump and forced back into the oil tank for re-circulation. Only one filter is incorporated in the D.S. lubrication system. It is of the gauze type and is included in the feed side of the oil circuit. It is fitted to the adaptor screwed into the oil tank.

Suitable Engine Oils. Top-up the oil tank regularly about every 200 miles to the correct level (half to three-quarters full). The brands and grades

of engine oils recommended by Norton Motors Ltd., for all S.V. and O.H.V. Nortons are—
1. Castrol XXL (summer) or XL (winter).
2. Shell X-100 40 (summer) or X-100 30 (winter).
3. Mobiloil BB (summer) or A (winter).
4. Essolube 40 (summer) or Essolube 30 (winter).

During the running-in period it is beneficial to mix colloidal graphite with the engine oil (*see* page 9). Note that if this compound is used for a longer period, the amount used should be reduced by half.

Concerning Engine Lubrication. Very little attention indeed is required on 1955 and later dry-sump models, and if the following instructions are carefully followed it is unlikely that any trouble will be experienced. See that the oil tank is always kept half to three-quarters full or on later models at or near the level of the transfer on the outside of the tank. Before checking the level in the tank run the engine for a few minutes. By doing this all surplus oil in the crankcase is scavenged by the pump and returned to the tank. It is possible for some oil to siphon through the return gears to the sump after the engine has been allowed to remain stationary for some time.

To check the oil circulation, remove the tank-filler cap and observe the oil being ejected from the oil return pipe. Note that after the engine has been running for several minutes, the oil flow becomes spasmodic because of the greater capacity of the oil-pump return gears, compared with the gears on the feed side. Top-up the oil tank about every 200 miles.

Upper cylinder lubrication is not necessary but sometimes beneficial; 1955 and later engines have no adjustment provided in the D.S. lubrication system, other than in regard to the oil-pressure control valve.

The Oil-pressure Control Valve. It is inadvisable to remove the ball from the valve unless there is reason to think that the ball is failing to seat, or is sticking. At the Norton Works the ball spring adjusting-screw is screwed right home and then released $1\frac{1}{2}$ threads. Do not tamper with this adjustment unnecessarily. Incidentally, there is no other adjustment provided in the lubrication system. If for any reason the oil-pressure control valve is dismantled, the correct order of assembly is: the ball itself; the spring; the adjuster nut. Tighten the latter fully and then screw it out $1\frac{1}{2}$ turns. Afterwards lock it with a centre-punch.

Drain the Oil Tank Every 2,000 Miles. On Norton engines with D.S. lubrication, the oil tank should be emptied and flushed out, the filter cleaned with paraffin, and the oil changed at least once every 2,000 miles. In the case of a new or rebored engine do this after the first 500 miles' running.

On 1955–8 models drain the tank, with the oil warm, by removing the

LUBRICATION 35

base plug. Do not lose its washer, and use a large receptacle to avoid an unnecessary mess.

On 1959 and later models the filter need not be removed when the oil is changed. It is preferable to remove the oil tank complete from the motor-cycle and wash out the tank thoroughly at, say, every second or third oil change. The filter is then automatically cleaned without removal and does not have its joint disturbed. Should it be necessary to remove it, with a ring spanner remove the rubber or plastic pipe.

Note that the filter occupies a higher position in the tank than does the drain plug and therefore small particles of foreign matter are trapped in the bottom of the tank until such time as the drain plug is removed.

Drain Crankcase When Decarbonizing. Drain the crankcase after the first 500 miles and when decarbonizing. Do this when the engine is warm. It is unnecessary on all 1955 and later engines to flush out the crankcase, because a sludge trap is provided. When the crankcase drain-plug is removed, all sludge comes away.

Rocker-box Lubrication. Automatic lubrication of the rocker-box is to be found on all 1955 and later O.H.V. engines, and apart from the optional use of upper-cylinder lubricant mixed with the petrol, no attention by the rider is necessary.

Lubrication of a Lucas "Magdyno" (1955–8). The bearings of the machine are packed with grease before a new model leaves the works, and this is quite sufficient until a complete overhaul is necessary when the "Magdyno" unit should be stripped down by a Lucas service agent and the bearings repacked with grease, and the instrument given any other attention that is necessary.

About every 2,500 miles insert a few drops of thin machine-oil on the wick in the contact-breaker base. The wick is carried by a small screw and to remove this screw it is first necessary to remove the spring arm carrying the moving contact (*see* Fig. 28), when the wick screw can be withdrawn.

When replacing the spring arm carrying the outer contact, see that the small backing spring is correctly located on the *outside* of the spring arm, with the curved portion facing *outwards*. Replace the spring washer and securing screw, and tighten the latter firmly.

If occasion is had to remove the complete contact-breaker, it is a good plan to push out the tappet from the contact-breaker body and smear this tappet with a little thin machine-oil.

Lubrication of Contact-breaker Unit (1959–62). *See* page 28.

THE MOTOR-CYCLE PARTS

Four-speed Gearbox Lubrication. Suitable lubricant for the 1955 and later four-speed Burman or AMC gearbox is engine oil, preferably of summer grade (*see* page 34). The correct level of lubricant in the four-speed gearbox is such that the layshaft is half submerged (i.e., the gearbox is about *one-third* full). An original charge of ½ pint of engine oil is advised and subsequent topping-up about every 1,000 miles should thereafter be adequate. Do not forget to lubricate the clutch control about once every 1,000 miles.

When topping-up the gearbox, pour engine oil into the filler-plug hole, or use an oil-gun, until the oil level reaches the hole or level plug hole. Rotation with the kick-starter will facilitate replenishment. Drain and refill the gearbox every 5,000 miles. When replenishing the gearbox, always allow ample time for the oil to find its natural level.

The Primary Chain. On 1955–62 models replenish the oil-bath chain case about every 1,000 miles with engine oil (*see* page 34). It is advisable to use Wakefield's "Castrolite," Shell X–100 20, Price's Energol SAE 20, Essolube 20, Havoline 20 or Mobiloil Arctic. To replenish, remove the inspection cover *A* from the chain case (Fig. 20) and also the oil-level plug *B* from the base of the chain case. Then pour oil through the inspection-cover hole until it reaches the oil-level plug hole with the motor-cycle upright. Drain and refill every 10,000 miles.

The Secondary Chain. On 1955–58 models brush on graphite grease every 1,000 miles. Engine oil can be used for the chain also, and in this case the best method of lubricating the chain is to rotate it, with the wheel, and apply an oil-gun or an oil-can to the lower chain run. See that the oil is falling upon the bearing surfaces and not merely on the rollers, and lubricate whenever the chain seems to be running dry. If chain lubrication is insufficient, undue wear of the chain and sprockets will occur, and the transmission may become somewhat harsh.

Every 3,500 miles (especially on earlier models) remove the chain and submerge it in paraffin. If the chain is allowed to soak well, all the dirt will be extracted. Hang the chain up to dry and replace it. Before doing this, however, it is a good plan to immerse the chain in a receptacle containing a quantity of warm chain lubricant containing graphite. This will penetrate to all the bearing surfaces.

On 1959 and later Nortons the secondary chain is automatically lubricated by oil mist from a crankcase breather or oil tank vent pipe but it also requires occasional cleaning and greasing. Castrolease Graphited is a good grease.

The Steering Head. Grease the ball bearings in the steering head every 2,000 miles by applying the grease-gun to the nipples where provided.

Suitable Greases. Suitable greases to use for all grease-gun points on the machine are: Castrol "Castrolease" Medium, BP Energrease C3,

Shell Retinax A, Mobilgrease MP, Esso Multi-Purpose grease, or Regent "Marfak" Multi-Purpose 2 grease. When using the grease gun, make sure that it is adequately filled, and try it out before applying it.

FIG. 20. NEAR-SIDE VIEW OF O.H.V. MODEL SHOWING OIL-BATH CHAIN CASE (1955–8)

A. Inspection cover
B. Oil-level plug
C. Nipple for rear-brake pedal

Replenishing the Telescopic Front Forks. "Roadholder" telescopic-type front forks with hydraulic damping are fitted as standard to all 1955 and later Nortons. These require to be replenished with damping oil about every 5,000 miles on 1955–8 models and about every 10,000 miles on 1959–62 models. Suitable damping oils are: Wakefield's "Castrolite," Shell

X–100 20, or B.P. Energol SAE 20, Mobiloil "Arctic," Essolube 20, or Advanced Havoline 20.

To replenish the forks on 1955–8 models, first remove the hexagon-headed filler plug from the top of each fork leg. Then remove the drain plug from each fork-end and allow all damping oil to drain out. Complete draining is assisted by operating the forks manually a few times. Replace the two drain plugs and replenish each fork leg with a measured *quarter of a pint* of one of the above-mentioned damping oils. Afterwards operate the forks several times to eliminate air-locks, and finally replace the two filler plugs.

The 1959–62 Telescopic Forks. These front forks (*see* Fig. 64) are of different design to the 1955–8 forks (*see* Fig. 63), but the same type of damping oils referred to above are suitable. The damping oil should be replenished at approximately 10,000-mile intervals, or whenever the normal characteristics of the forks appear to have deteriorated. Where a new machine is concerned it is advisable to change the damping oil after covering about 1,000 miles. Any swarf or other metal particles collected during the bedding-in period can then be cleaned out.

Each fork leg has a drain plug consisting of a cheese-head screw. Place a suitable receptacle on the ground and remove the two drain plugs, one at a time. Be careful not to lose the small aluminium or fibre washer which makes the seal. Next hold the front brake on and move the forks up and down to expel the damping oil. Drain for a few minutes and repeat on the other side. Now refit the drain plugs with their washers and place the machine on its centre stand.

Unscrew the large filler plug on the top of each fork leg and "pull up" the front wheel to expose the springs. Place a block of wood or similar obstruction beneath the wheel to hold the springs clear. Then with two spanners unscrew the filler plug nuts from the top of the damper rods. Remove the wood block and permit the forks to fully extend. Now pour in a measured 5 fluid ounces (142 c.c.) of damping oil into each fork leg. Because the telescopic forks have springs inside the main tubes the damping oil is slow to run down and some patience is therefore required when refilling.

It is most important before refitting the filler plugs to the damper rods to make quite sure that their lock-nuts are screwed down to the end of the thread on the rod. Lock the two together and screw in, and tighten the filler plugs.

Wheel Hubs (1955–6). On both the front and rear wheels, nipples are provided, and the hubs should each be injected with 3–4 strokes of the grease-gun about every 1,000 miles. Do not use excessive grease, or it may get on the brake linings and reduce brake efficiency. Use one of the greases mentioned on page 36. It is most important to keep the bearings of all wheels well greased, as they perform heavy duties. On a sidecar outfit, do not forget to grease the bearings of the sidecar wheel.

Wheels Hubs (1957-62). About every 10,000 miles remove both wheels, dismantle the hubs and repack the bearings with grease.

Brakes. Grease the brake pedal shaft (C, Fig. 20), the brake shoes cams, and the brake-cam spindles every 2,000 miles. Appropriate nipples are provided. Oil the exposed front-brake cable and the rear-brake rod joints at the same time.

Control Levers. Apply the oil-can every 1,000 miles to the cables where they are apt to bind on the control mechanism on the handlebars. Oil all linkage pins and also the nipples. When fitting new cables and casings, charge the latter with grease. A length of rubber tube can be used in conjunction with the grease-gun to inject grease.

The Rear Springing. On 1955 and later models with "swinging arm" rear suspension no lubrication or other maintenance is necessary. The oil-damped units are leak-proof, and normally no attempt should be made to dismantle, drain, or replenish the suspension units. Do not lubricate the "swinging arm" pivot which has "Silentbloc" bushes or "Clayflex" bearings.

Miscellaneous. Every 3,000 miles grease the speedometer-drive gearbox. On 1955-8 "Magdyno" models oil the commutator end bracket where provision for lubrication is provided. On 1959 and subsequent coil-ignition models attend to the automatic ignition advance mechanism (*see* page 28).

CHAPTER V

THE AMAL CARBURETTOR

ALL Nortons are sent out from the works with their carburettors carefully tuned and with jet sizes giving the best all-round performance. It is not wise to alter the maker's setting, but sometimes it is disturbed and requires adjustment. The carburettor fitted to all 1955 and later Norton engines is

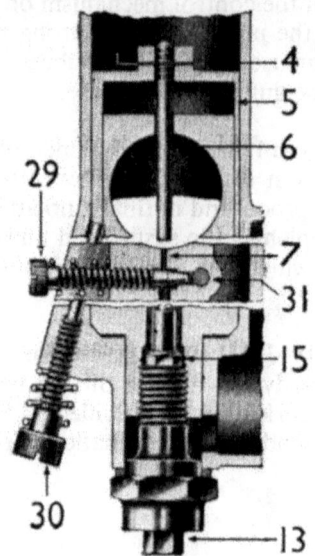

FIG. 21. THROTTLE-STOP AND PILOT-AIR ADJUSTING SCREWS
For key to numbered parts, *see* page 42.

of the two-lever needle-jet type, the mixture at slow or idling speeds being controlled by a readily adjustable pilot jet, whilst at higher speeds the mixture is controlled by means of a needle attached to the throttle slide and working in a restriction jet.

VITAL PARTS

The Throttle Stop. The throttle-stop screw is normally adjusted to prop the throttle slide open sufficiently to enable the engine to tick-over nicely when the twist-grip is closed. The design of the throttle-stop screw on the carburettor fitted to 1955–62 O.H.V. Nortons is shown in Fig. 21.

The Pilot Air Screw. This controls the suction imposed on the pilot jet by controlling the volume of air which mixes with the fuel. It controls the strength of the mixture for "idling" and also for initial throttle openings (up to one-eighth throttle).

The Main Jet. This regulates the fuel supply at throttle openings exceeding three-quarters full open. At smaller openings of the throttle, the fuel supplied passes through the main jet, but the amount is decreased owing to the needle in the needle-jet having a controlling effect. The main jet is screwed into the needle-jet and can readily be detached after removing the main-jet cover (12 in Fig. 22).

Each Amal main jet is numbered and calibrated so that its precise discharge is known. It thus follows that any two main jets having the same number are identical in all respects. The larger the jet, the higher is its number. If a larger size jet is needed, on no account attempt to ream the existing jet, but obtain a new one of larger size. Recommended jet sizes are given in Table I.

The Needle and Needle-jet. The jet needle is attached to, and moves with, the throttle slide. Being tapered, it permits more or less fuel to pass through the needle-jet as the throttle is opened, or closed, respectively. This applies throughout the range of throttle openings, except at nearly full throttle and when "idling." The needle-jet is of a specified size, and normally it should not be changed except when going over to alcohol fuels for racing.

As may be seen in Fig. 21, the position of the taper needle, relative to the throttle opening, can be adjusted according to the mixture required, by securing the needle to the throttle with the needle spring-clip in a particular groove, *five* of which are provided. Position No. 3, for example, means the third groove *from the top*. At throttle openings from one-quarter to three-quarters open, raising the needle enriches the mixture, while lowering the needle weakens it. The needle itself is made in *one size only*.

The Throttle-valve Cut-away. The throttle valve on the atmospheric side is cut away, and this affects the depression on the main fuel supply. The cut-away provides a means of tuning between the pilot and needle-jet range of throttle opening. The actual amount of cut-away is denoted by a number marked on the throttle slide. Thus 6/4 means a throttle type 6 with a No. 4 cut-away. A throttle with a larger cut-away (say, 6/5) *weakens* the mixture. A smaller cut-away, on the other hand, makes the mixture *richer*.

HOW IT WORKS (1955 ONWARDS)

Details of the Amal "monobloc" carburettor are shown in Figs. 21 and 22-3, and the accompanying key to these four sectional views indicates

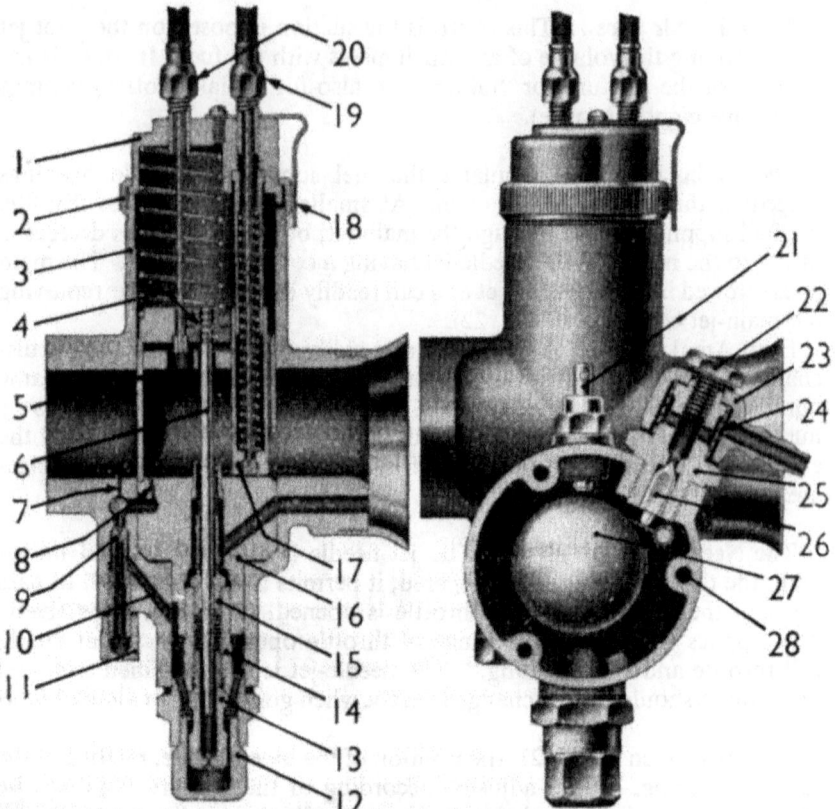

FIGS. 22, 23. SECTIONS THROUGH (LEFT) MIXING CHAMBER AND (RIGHT) FLOAT CHAMBER OF AMAL "MONOBLOC" CARBURETTOR (1955 ONWARDS)

KEY TO FIGS. 21, 22–3

1. Mixing-chamber top
2. Mixing-chamber cap
3. Body of carburettor
4. Jet-needle clip
5. Throttle valve
6. Jet needle
7. Pilot outlet
8. Pilot by-pass
9. Pilot jet
10. Feed to pilot jet
11. Pilot-jet cover nut
12. Main-jet cover
13. Main jet
14. Main-jet holder
15. Needle-jet
16. Jet block
17. Air valve
18. Retaining spring for 2
19. Cable adjuster (air)
20. Cable adjuster (throttle)
21. Tickler
22. Banjo bolt
23. Banjo
24. Filter gauze
25. Needle seating
26. Float-chamber needle
27. Float (hinged)
28. Float-chamber cover screws
29. Pilot-air adjusting screw
30. Throttle-stop adjusting screw
31. Air passage to pilot jet
32. Feed holes in 9
33. "Bleed" holes in 15
34. Primary air choke
35. Primary air passage
36. Throttle-valve cut-away

all the essential parts. Basically, the carburettor works on the same general principles as the earlier type with a vertical and separate float chamber, non-detachable pilot jet, and needle-jet of the non-compensating type.

Referring to Figs. 22–4, the float 27 maintains a constant level of petrol in the needle-jet 15 and the pilot jet 9, and it cuts off the petrol supply when the engine stops.

The selection of the appropriate jet sizes and main choke bore ensures

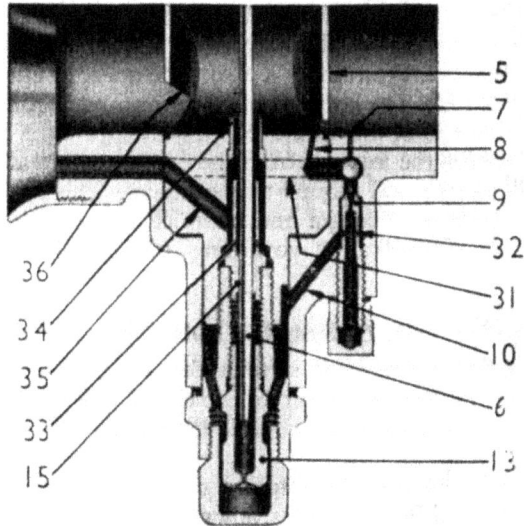

FIG. 24. DIAGRAMMATIC SECTION THROUGH AMAL "MONOBLOC" CARBURETTOR (1955 ONWARDS)

Illustrating only the lower half of the throttle chamber and the internal primary air passages to the main jet and pilot system. The throttle valve is shown slightly open.

the proper atomizing and proportioning of the petrol and air sucked into the engine. The air valve is normally kept fully raised and the throttle valve (controlled by the handlebar twist-grip) controls the volume of mixture and therefore the power; at all throttle openings a correct mixture is automatically obtained. The carburettor operates in four stages.

When opening the throttle from the fully closed position to one-eighth open (for idling) the mixture is supplied by the pilot jet, and mixture strength is determined by the setting of the knurled pilot-air adjusting screw (see Fig. 21). To facilitate adjustment of this screw a coil spring is used instead of a lock-nut. As the throttle is opened farther the main-jet system comes into action, the mixture being augmented from the main jet 13 via the pilot by-pass 8.

The amount of cut-away on the atmospheric side of the throttle valve regulates the petrol-air ratio between one-eighth and one-quarter throttle. The needle-jet 15 and the jet needle 6 take over mixture regulation between one-quarter and three-quarter throttle, and mixture strength is determined by the vertical position of the needle in the clip 4 attached to the throttle valve 5. When the throttle is opened beyond three-quarter, the mixture strength is decided only by the size of the main jet.

Note that the main jet 13 does not spray petrol direct into the carburettor mixing-chamber but petrol discharges through the needle-jet into the primary air chamber. From there it enters the main air choke through the primary air choke 34. The latter has a compensating action in conjunction with "bleed" holes 33 in the needle-jet 15, which serve the double purpose of air compensating the mixture from the needle-jet and allowing the fuel to form a well outside and around the needle-jet. This is always available for snap acceleration. Pilot-jet and main-jet behaviour are not affected by this two-way compensation governing only acceleration and normal cruising.

TUNING THE CARBURETTOR (1955 ONWARDS)

The correct Amal carburettor settings for all 1955–62 Norton single-cylinder O.H.V. models are given in Table I. Do not alter these settings (decided by the makers after careful deliberation) without very good reasons.

Note that it is desirable to obtain a slightly weak mixture consistent with good slow-running; an excessively rich slow-running mixture causes a tendency for the engine to run on the pilot jet under normal running conditions. The effect of this is to increase the fuel consumption. To modify the strength of the running mixture, it is necessary to make an adjustment to the position of the jet needle in the throttle valve, or else to alter the size of the main jet.

Colour of the Exhaust Flame. Where the carburettor is correctly tuned, there should be no evidence of black smoke. The combustion of fuel is complete and carbon formation almost non-existent. If the mixture is right, the exhaust flame is of a *whitish-blue* colour.

If the mixture is weak, the colour of the exhaust flame is *light blue*. If, on the other hand, the mixture is excessively rich, the flame is of a characteristic *yellow* colour, and some *black* smoke is generally present. Note that the above references to exhaust flames imply exhaust flames observed at an *open* exhaust port.

Tuning Procedure. If the carburettor setting (*see* Table I) does not give complete satisfaction for particular requirements, there are four separate

Table I
CARBURETTOR SETTINGS FOR O.H.V.
SINGLE-CYLINDER MODELS (1955–62)

Model (Norton)	Pilot Jet	Main Jet Size	Throttle Valve	Needle Position
ES2 (1955–8)	30	270	376/4	3
ES2 (1955–9)	30	270	3	3
ES2 (1960–2)	30	270	4	3
19 (1955–8)	30	270	376/4	3
50 (1955–62)	30	210	376/3½	2

ways of rectifying matters as given herewith, and the adjustments should be made in this order—
1. Main jet ($\frac{3}{4}$ to full throttle).
2. Pilot air adjustment (closed to $\frac{1}{8}$ throttle).
3. Throttle-valve cut-away on the air intake side ($\frac{1}{8}$ to $\frac{1}{4}$ throttle).
4. Needle position ($\frac{1}{4}$ to $\frac{3}{4}$ throttle).

The diagram (Fig. 25) clearly indicates the part of the throttle range over which each adjustment is effective.

The carburettor is, throughout the throttle range, entirely automatic, and the air lever should be kept wide open, except for starting from cold and until the engine has warmed up properly. It is assumed that normal petrol is used for tuning, which should be done in the sequence described below. Throttle openings to be used in the five tuning operations are those indicated in Fig. 25. By following these tuning instructions (which have been recommended by Amal Ltd.) you will be assured of the most satisfactory performance with maximum economy of fuel. For tuning purposes it is advisable to start up on a quiet road having a slight up-gradient, so as to impose a small load on the engine.

1. To Check Size of the Main Jet. Accelerate up to full throttle and carefully note the response of the engine to twist-grip action. Should power output appear better with the air lever very slightly closed or with the throttle not completely open, this indicates that the main jet is too small, and the next larger size should be tried. Similarly, if there is a tendency for the engine to run "heavily" on full throttle, this denotes that the main jet is too large and the next smaller size should be experimented with.*

If tuning for speed, be careful to choose a main jet of size sufficient to maintain the engine in a cool condition. Make a run at high speed, pull

---
* Different size jets are obtainable from Amal spares stockists, or from Amal Ltd., Holdford Road, Witton, Birmingham, 6.

up, and stop the engine immediately. Remove the sparking plug and closely inspect it. If the business end of the plug is sooty, the mixture is too rich. Should the body be dry grey in colour, the mixture is on the weak side, and a larger size jet is required.

With a properly proportioned mixture, the plug body should have a bright black appearance. Also, when running, observe the sound of the exhaust; it should be crisp and have no trace of "woolliness," Black smoke at the exhaust shows that the mixture is much too rich.

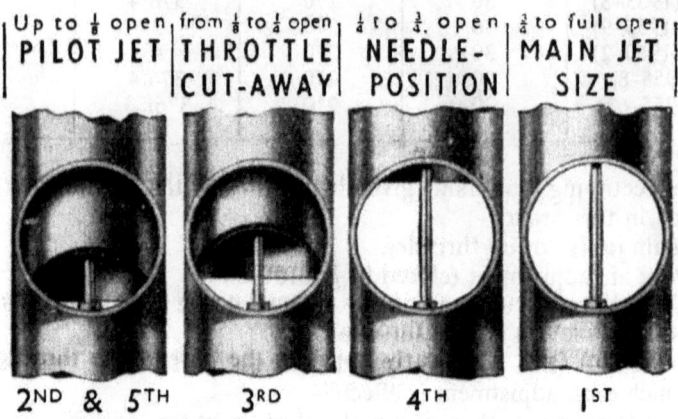

FIG. 25. RANGE AND SEQUENCE OF TUNING—
AMAL CARBURETTOR

2. **To Adjust the Pilot Jet (1955 Onwards).** Start up the engine. Allow it to run idle at an excessive speed, with the throttle twist-grip closed and the throttle slide abutting the throttle-stop screw (Fig. 21). Open the air lever wide open and retard the ignition lever (1955–9 models) to obtain the best slow-running.

Unscrew the throttle stop-screw until the engine slows up and begins to stall. Then screw the pilot-air screw in or out as required to enable the engine to run regularly and faster. To weaken the mixture, screw the pilot-air adjuster screw *outwards*.

Next gently lower the throttle-stop screw until the engine again begins to falter. Now commence to readjust the pilot-air adjuster screw to obtain the optimum slow-running. Should this second adjustment cause the engine to tick-over at an excessive speed, repeat the adjustment a third time.

3. **The Throttle Cut-away.** Should appreciable spitting-back at the carburettor occur on accelerating from rest* with the engine idling, stop

* Rev the engine up and down sharply several times and note whether the exhaust is nice and crisp, with no "flat spots" as the twist-grip is rotated. It is essential to obtain good acceleration as well as good tick-over.

the machine and slightly enrich the mixture by screwing the pilot-air screw in approximately *half a turn*. If this does not effect the desired result, screw it back to its former position and fit a throttle slide having a smaller cut-away.

If there is no spitting-back but the engine jerks under load, this shows an over-rich mixture, and the remedy is to fit a throttle slide with larger cut-away, or else to lower the throttle needle one notch.

4. The Jet-needle Position. The tapered jet-needle influences a wide range of throttle openings and affects acceleration. Check performance with the needle in as low a position as possible, i.e. with the clip in the groove nearest the end of the needle. If acceleration declines, and improves by partially closing the air lever, raise the position of the needle by two grooves. If a marked improvement is thereby obtained, try the effect of lowering the needle, by one groove, and leave it in the position where the best performance is obtained.

It should be noted that if the mixture is still excessively rich with the needle clip in groove No. 1 (nearest the end), wear of the needle-jet has probably occurred and renewal of the jet is called for. The needle itself is of stainless steel and wear does not take place, even after a big mileage.

5. Verify the Idling Adjustment. Also make any final small adjustment to obtain a perfectly smooth tick-over, neither too fast nor too slow.

Possible Causes of Bad Slow-running. If it is found impossible to obtain good slow-running by making the pilot air adjustment as described in paragraph 2 on page 46, it is possible there are air leaks, due to a poor joint at the carburettor attachment to the cylinder and/or a worn inlet valve guide. Badly seating valves will also weaken the mixture. Defects in the ignition system may also be responsible for poor tick-over. The sparking plug may be oily, or the points set too close (*see* page 52). Possibly the spark is excessively advanced or the contact-breaker needs attention (*see* pages 28, 55). Examine the slip-ring for oil and see that the pick-up brush is bedding down and in good condition. Also examine the h.t. cable for signs of shorting.

The Pilot Jet Obstructed. If the pilot-jet adjustment does not obtain the desired results and the engine will not idle nicely with the throttle almost closed, the air lever adjusted wide open, and the ignition half to two-thirds advanced, (1955-8) it is possible that the pilot jet is obstructed.

On 1955 and later models it is only necessary to remove the pilot-jet cover nut 11 below the choke body (*see* Fig. 22) and unscrew the pilot jet for inspection and cleaning. The correct jet is a No. 30.

High Fuel Consumption. If, in spite of careful checking of the tuning of the carburettor, high fuel consumption continues, it is likely that one or more of the following causes is responsible. Late ignition timing will eat into your petrol supplies quickly. The same applies to poor engine compression due to badly fitting piston rings or badly seated valves. Also take into consideration the question of flooding due to a faulty float chamber, air leakage at the joint between the carburettor and engine, or weak valve springs. See that no wastage is caused by slack petrol-pipe union nuts.

MAINTENANCE

Stripping Down Carburettor (1955 Onwards). To remove the "monobloc" carburettor for dismantling and cleaning, first turn off the petrol and disconnect the fuel pipe from the float-chamber union. Remove both nuts securing the carburettor flange to the cylinder head and unscrew the knurled cap on top of the mixing chamber. The air and throttle slides can be withdrawn, during or after detaching the carburettor. Do not remove the carburettor slides unless cable or slide renewal is called for.

Referring to Figs. 22–4, dismantling the carburettor is very straightforward. To remove the jet needle 6, withdraw the jet-needle clip 4 on top of the throttle valve 5.

To obtain access to the float 27, remove the three screws 28 securing the cover to the float chamber. Lift out the hinged float 27 and withdraw the moulded-nylon needle 26. Lay both aside for cleaning.

The float-chamber vent is incorporated in the tickler 21, and the top-feed union houses a filter element of fine gauze which is readily accessible for cleaning. To remove the filter gauze, unscrew the banjo bolt 22, remove the banjo 23, and also the gauze.

To remove the main jet 13, remove the main-jet cover 12 and unscrew the jet from the jet holder 14. Remove the jet block locating screw to the left of and slightly below the pilot-air adjusting screw 29. Then push or tap out the jet block 16 through the larger end of the mixing chamber body. To remove the pilot jet it is only necessary to remove the pilot-jet cover nut 11 and unscrew the jet.

Cleaning. Wash all components thoroughly clean with petrol. Pay special attention to the float chamber, and see that any impurities collected inside are removed completely. Clean the gauze filter occasionally ("monobloc" carburettor), and blow all ducts clear.

Inspection. If the carburettor has been in continuous service for a considerable period, inspect the following—

1. FLOAT CHAMBER. Scrutinize the components closely.

In the case of the "monobloc" carburettor, check that the joint faces of the float-chamber cover and float chamber are not bruised or damaged, and that the joint washer is sound, otherwise it will be difficult to obtain a petrol-tight joint. See that the filter is undamaged.

THE AMAL CARBURETTOR 49

2. THROTTLE VALVE. Test in the mixing chamber, and if excessive play is present it is advisable to renew the valve without delay.

3. THROTTLE NEEDLE CLIP. This part must securely grip the needle. Free rotation must *not* take place, otherwise the needle groove will become worn and necessitate a new part being fitted. Be sure to refit the clip in the correct groove.

4. JET BLOCK. If trouble has been experienced with erratic "idling," ascertain by blowing that the pilot jet is clear, and that the pilot outlet in the mixing chamber is unobstructed.

5. CARBURETTOR FLANGE (1955–62). Occasionally check the flange face of the "monobloc" carburettor for truth. Slight distortion sometimes occurs after a considerable mileage. The remedy is to file and rub down the face on emery cloth laid on a surface plate, until a straight-edge shows the face surface to be dead flat. Better still, grind the face.

To Reassemble Carburettor (1955 Onwards). Assemble the instrument in the reverse order of dismantling. Note the following items (*see* Figs. 22, 23). Verify that the washer fitted to the bottom of the jet block 16 is in sound condition. Check the condition also of the washer fitted to the main-jet holder 14, and renew the washer if not perfect. When replacing the throttle valve 5, make sure that the tapered jet-needle does actually enter the hole in the centre of the jet block. Check that the throttle slide moves freely when the mixing-chamber cap 2 is screwed down firmly and held by the retaining spring 18.

When replacing the float 27 in the float chamber, see that the narrower side of the hinge is *uppermost*. Be sure that the joint faces of the float chamber and cover are clean and undamaged. This is important, otherwise petrol leakage may occur. See that the petrol-filter gauze is sound and quite clean (*see* page 48). Before replacing the banjo 23, turn on the petrol tap for a second and observe that petrol flows freely. Make certain that both the nuts securing the carburettor flange to the light-alloy cylinder head are tightened *evenly* and firmly. Avoid using a large spanner for final tightening. The washer at this joint must be perfectly sound. A thick washer should not be used.

To Dismantle Twist-grip and Air Lever. *See* pages 80, 81.

CHAPTER VI

GENERAL MAINTENANCE

ALL essential instructions are included in this chapter for the routine maintenance, dismantling and assembling of 1955–62 O.H.V. single-cylinder Nortons. In 1955 S.V. engines were dropped, and light-alloy heads fitted to all O.H.V. singles. In 1959 coil ignition was fitted.

In this chapter most of the O.H.V. maintenance instructions are clearly dated, but note that *where no dating is given, the instructions concerned apply to 1955 onwards.*

Norton Spares. When ordering spare parts always remember to quote the type of machine, its year of manufacture, and Engine No. or Frame No. (*see* below). Spares can be obtained from any of the numerous Norton spares stockists.

Large firms (some having many branches) handling general tools, accessories, clothing, etc., include: The Halford Cycle Co. Ltd.; Marble Arch Motor Supplies Ltd.; Turner's Stores; George Grose Ltd.; Pride & Clarke Ltd.; Whitbys of Acton Ltd.; Claude Rye Ltd.; E.S. Motors; and James Grose Ltd.

The Engine and Frame Numbers. You will find the engine number of your mount on the *transmission side of the crankcase* below the cylinder base flange. The frame number is stamped on *the head lug of the frame,* below the steering damper anchor-plate, *or on later models on the left-hand frame gusset below the battery box.*

TOOLS, ETC.

Items Needed for Maintenance. Items which you must have for the *engine* include: a tin of suitable engine oil (*see* page 33), a drip-tray, a suitable receptacle for draining oil from the oil tank and crankcase, a can of paraffin for cleaning purposes, a stiff brush for scouring dirt from the under side of the engine, some non-fluffy rags, some dishes and jars in which to wash components, a tin of medium-grade valve grinding paste, such as Richford's, some fine emery cloth, some wood or metal boxes in which to store parts pending assembly, a rubber suction-type (or a metal type) valve holder (for O.H.V. engines), a valve spring compressor (*see* page 71), a pair of gudgeon-pin circlips, a set of engine gaskets, some insulation tape, a small wire brush and a good set of feeler gauges for checking the contact-breaker and plug gaps, and a plug regapping tool (*see* Fig. 26).

For the maintenance of the *motor-cycle* parts you will need: a canister of suitable grease (*see* page 36), an oil-can, a small funnel for topping-up the gearbox, a good tyre repair outfit, a tyre pressure gauge (*see* page 4), a box of spare chain links, a proprietary chain rivet extractor, a bottle containing distilled water, a Lucas battery filler (a hydrometer is also desirable), a sponge and pail (where no hose is available), a chamois leather, some soft dusters, some rags (old shirts will do), some good polish for the enamelled parts, and last, but by no means least, some good hands cleanser. If you are an all-weather rider, it is advisable to obtain some cleaning compound (such as "Gunk") for the machine. The kit supplied with each brand new Norton should be sufficient for all normal stripping down and maintenance work. It includes essential tools and a grease-gun for greasing motor-cycle parts.

The standard Norton tool-kit for O.H.V. models does not include an adjustable spanner, nor a pair of pliers. The former is useful and a small pair of snipe-nose pliers is *necessary* when removing a gudgeon-pin circlip in order to remove the piston from the connecting-rod.

Cleaning the Chromium. Never employ liquid metal polish or paste, as this will wear down the thin surface. A good chromium-cleaning compound can, however, safely be used. The normal method of removing tarnish (salt deposits) is to clean the surfaces regularly with a damp chamois leather and then polish them with soft dusters.

To Reduce Tarnishing. During the winter months it is a good plan to wipe over occasionally all surfaces with a soft cloth soaked in a proprietary anti-tarnish preparation. An example is "Tekall," obtainable in ½ pint and 1 pint tins.

Cleaning the Engine and Gearbox. See that the cylinder barrel and cylinder-head fins are kept clean and black (except alloy heads). If the enamel has worn away, paint the fins with some proprietary cylinder black after thorough cleaning with a stiff brush dipped in paraffin. Note that rusted fins, besides looking shabby, cause an appreciable loss in heat dispersion.

Scour off all filth from the lower part of the engine and gearbox with stiff brushes and paraffin. Clean all aluminium alloy and bright surfaces with a rag damped in paraffin, assisted by brushes where necessary.

To Clean the Enamel. Never attempt to remove mud from the enamelled parts when dry and caked, as this is likely to damage the surfaces. Soak the mud off with a hose if available. In the case of a very dirty machine it may be advisable to paint the surfaces over with a cleaning compound such as "Gunk" before directing a stream of water on to the dirty surfaces. Be careful not to allow any water to get inside vulnerable parts such as the "Magdyno" and carburettor. If a hose is not available, soak the mud and then disperse it with plenty of clean water, using a sponge and pail.

Having removed all dirt, dry the enamelled surfaces with a chamois leather and afterwards polish them with soft dusters and some good wax polish or a proprietary polish such as "Karpol."

"Dry weather" riders can keep a machine in almost showroom condition merely by rubbing the enamel over with a paraffin-damped rag, followed by a dry, soft duster.

Run-in a New Engine Carefully. Go very steady during the first 1,000 miles and put into practice the important advice given on page 9. Avoid large throttle openings and make full use of the gearbox.

Check Nuts for Tightness. This is particularly important during running-in, as some "bedding down" of parts invariably occurs. Regularly apply spanners to the various external nuts to ensure tightness, paying special attention to the engine bolts and nuts, the engine mounting nuts, and the pipe unions. After running-in, make a regular check once a month, but after decarbonizing and running for a short mileage, check the cylinder-head nuts for tightness.

Obtaining Good Carburation. For hints on setting the controls for easy starting, *see* page 5. Chapter V tells you how the Amal "Monobloc" carburettor works and how to tune and clean it.

Correct Lubrication. For detailed instructions, *see* Chapter IV.

Care of Lighting Equipment. For instructions concerning the dynamo portion of the Lucas "Magdyno" used on 1955-8 models," the lamps, and the battery, refer to Chapter II. Wiring diagrams will be found on pages 22, 23, 30. For instructions on the maintenance of the lighting *and ignition system* on 1959-62 Models ES2, 50, *see* Chapter III.

SPARKING PLUGS AND THE LUCAS "MAGDYNO"

This section deals with the all-important sparking plug, and the ignition components of the Lucas "Magdyno" fitted to 1955-58 models. Ignition timing is covered on page 76.

Suitable Sparking Plugs. For the appropriate Lodge, K.L.G., and Champion plug recommendations *see* page 9.

Sparking Plug Gap. Difficult starting or occasional misfiring can usually be traced to a dirty or defective sparking plug. The life of a good plug is considerable, but the points of the electrodes gradually burn away and eventually the gap becomes enlarged considerably, and it is necessary to reset the points.

It is advisable to check the plug gap regularly (say every 2,000 miles) and to adjust the gap if burning of the points has caused the gap to exceed 0·022 in. Norton Motors, Ltd. recommend a gap of 0·020–0·022 in. For obvious reasons, when re-gapping it is advisable to set the gap at or near the *bottom* limit. Check the gap with a suitable feeler gauge. The gauge should just enter without springing the points.

When adjusting the plug gap, never attempt to bend or tap the centre electrode. Use a pair of snipe-nose pliers, or a plug regapping tool (shown

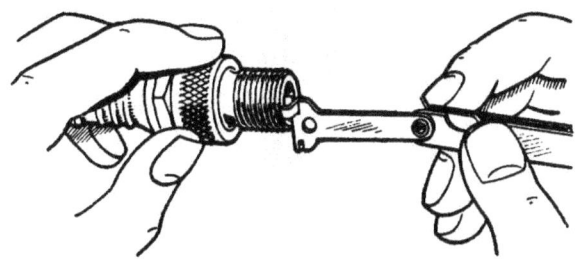

FIG. 26. A SAFE METHOD OF RE-GAPPING A PLUG
The Champion tool shown includes suitable gauges

in Fig. 26), to bend the outside (earth) electrode. Tapping the earth electrode is not a good method. When the plug has to be thoroughly cleaned, this should be done as described below, and the plug re-gapped *afterwards*.

Cleaning the Plug. If carburation is correct and excessive oil is not entering the combustion chamber, it should not be necessary to dismantle and clean the sparking plug thoroughly more often than once about every 3,000 miles. When running-in a new or rebored engine, it is advisable to remove and check the plug for cleanliness at intervals of about 500 miles.

Quick cleaning of a plug can be done by brushing the points and slightly rubbing their firing sides with some smooth emery cloth. Alternatively the plug can be cleaned with a proprietary gadget. Thorough cleaning (internal and external), however, is not possible without dismantling the plug (*see* below).

To Clean Lodge and K.L.G. Plugs Thoroughly. Fig 27 shows a typical detachable type (K.L.G.) sparking plug dismantled for thorough cleaning. To dismantle a detachable-type sparking plug, hold the smaller hexagon of the gland nut *B* lightly in a vice or with a suitable spanner. If you use a vice, be most careful not to exert any pressure on the hexagon faces. Then with a suitable spanner applied to the larger hexagon E of the plug body, unscrew the body until it is separated from the gland nut. The centre

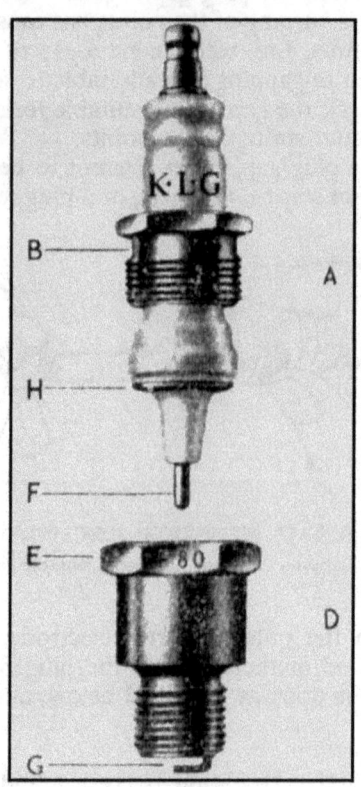

FIG. 27. DETACHABLE TYPE SPARKING PLUG (K.L.G.) DISMANTLED FOR THOROUGH CLEANING

The gland nut B and the internal washer H are shown still in position on the insulation.

electrode F with its insulation (comprising the insulated electrode assembly A) can now be detached from the gland nut. Take care not to lose the internal sealing washer H.

To clean the "Sintox" or "Corundite" insulation, used on Lodge and K.L.G. plugs respectively, wipe it clean with a cloth soaked in petrol or paraffin. If the insulation is coated with hard carbon deposits, remove these with some fine emery cloth, but make no attempt to scrape off the deposits. The internal sealing washer H and the surfaces on the insulator, and in the metal body on which this washer rests, are very important as they prevent gas leakage through the plug. Therefore wipe them only with a rag soaked in petrol or paraffin. Any damage caused while dismantling will render the plug unserviceable.

To clean the metal parts (plug body and gland nut), wipe them clean with petrol, or, if necessary, scrape off the deposits with a small knife, or use a wire brush. Afterwards rinse the parts in petrol. The gland nut seldom gets very fouled, but the inside of the plug body may be very dirty, and the same may apply to the external threads of the plug. Clean and polish the points of the centre and outside (earth) electrodes F and G (Fig. 27) with some fine emery cloth.

See that there is no dirt or grit lodged between the body of the plug and the insulation, and particularly on the internal sealing washer and the contacting faces. Smear a little thin oil on the internal washer and make sure that it seats properly. When assembling the sparking plug, see that the centre electrode and insulation are positioned centrally in the body bore. If it is not, remove, re-position by rotating the centre a quarter of a turn, and reassemble. Do not attempt to force it into position or bend it.

Avoid excessive tightening of the gland nut B. Finally verify that the plug gap is correct (*see* page 52).

To Clean Champion Plugs. To clean a non-detachable type Champion plug, take it to the nearest garage equipped with a Champion Service Unit. With this apparatus the plug can be cleaned in a few minutes of all deposits, washed, subjected to a high pressure air line, and tested for sparking on the Champion apparatus at an air pressure of over 100 lb per sq in.

Replacing Sparking Plug. Before replacing a plug, renew the copper washer if it is worn or flattened, and clean the plug threads with a wire brush. Screw the plug home by hand as far as possible, and always use the box spanner in the Norton tool kit for final tightening. An adjustable spanner should not be used, as this may cause distortion.

The "Magdyno" Contact-breaker Gap. Little attention to the ignition portion of the Lucas "Magdyno" is needed, other than occasional lubrication (*see* page 35) and attention to the face-cam type contact-breaker, shown in Fig. 28. Any serious internal trouble should be dealt with by a Lucas service agent.

The contacts of the contact-breaker (Fig. 28) should be examined on a new machine after the first 500 miles, and subsequently about every 2,500 miles. If the "break," with the contacts fully open is appreciably more, or less, than will just hold a 0·010–0·012 in. blade of a feeler gauge the contacts should be adjusted (*after* cleaning, if necessary). Too great a gap will advance the timing. The magneto-spanner gauge, or the blade of a proprietary set of feelers, can be useful for checking the "break," the procedure for which is as follows—

1. Remove the contact-breaker cover and rotate the engine slowly forwards until the contacts of the contact-breaker are wide open (i.e. near T.D.C. on the compression stroke).

2. Insert blade of the feeler gauge (0·010–0·012 in.) between the contacts.

3. If the feeler gauge *just* slides in without friction, the gap is correct and no adjustment is needed. If the gauge is a slack fit or the contacts have to be sprung to enable it to enter, adjust the gap as below.

4. With the magneto spanner loosen the lock-nut which secures the

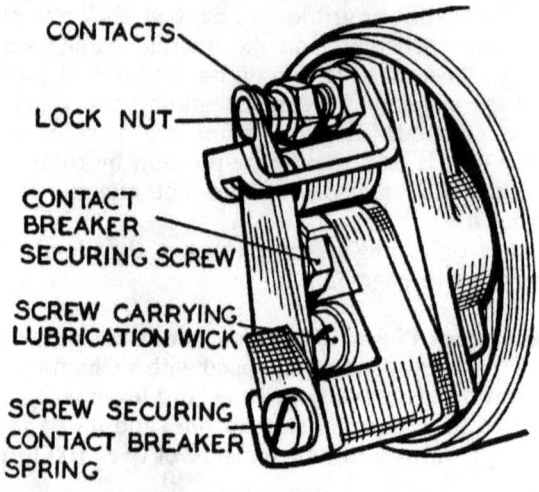

FIG. 28. THE FACE-CAM TYPE CONTACT-BREAKER ON THE LUCAS "MAGDYNO" (1955–58 MODELS)

adjustable contact screw (*see* Fig. 28) and then turn this screw by means of its hexagon head until the correct gap is obtained between the fixed and movable contacts.

5. Retighten the contact screw lock-nut and again check the gap. If correct, replace the contact-breaker cover.

Cleaning the "Magdyno" Contacts. At intervals of about 2,500 miles, when checking the contact-breaker gap, scrutinize the contacts closely. If the contacts are allowed to become dirty or oily, rapid burning, pitting, and consequent ignition trouble will ensue.

If inspection reveals that the contacts have a *grey, frosted* appearance, with no blackening or pitting, do not interfere with them (assuming that the gap is correct). If the contacts are only slightly discoloured, clean them with a rag moistened with petrol.

On examination after a big mileage the contacts may be found to have irregular and blackened areas due to pitting and burning (especially if the contacts have not been kept clean and correctly adjusted). In this case it is essential to clean them up, otherwise misfiring and rapid deterioration of the contacts will follow.

To clean the contacts, use a *fine* carborundum slip or a piece of *fine* emery cloth (do not use a nail file), and with the contact-breaker spring arm (*see* Fig. 28) removed, clean and polish the contacts until all pitting disappears and the contact surfaces are smooth all over. Be careful to keep the contact faces "square" as well as uniform. *This is most important.** If pitting is not appreciable it is permissible to insert the emery cloth between the two contacts, while both are in position. If pitting is serious, and in order to examine the contacts effectively, the spring arm must be removed. Remove any traces of rust from the arm.

To remove the spring arm (carrying the moving contact) on a face-cam type contact-breaker (*see* Fig. 28), it is only necessary to remove its securing screw and spring washer. When replacing the spring arm, make certain that the small backing spring is replaced immediately under the securing screw and spring washer, with the curved portion facing *outwards* as shown in Fig. 28. See that the contacts are perfectly aligned before tightening the securing screw.

Where very deep pitting is present, it may be necessary to remove the complete contact-breaker after detaching the spring arm. To do this, unlock the tab-washer and remove the contact-breaker securing screw, when the complete contact-breaker can be withdrawn, and dealt with on a bench or table if desired. When replacing the contact-breaker, see that a new tab-washer is fitted and locked over the securing screw. It is not advisable to remove much metal from the contacts, and if a reasonable amount of facing up fails to restore the surfaces to normal, fit a new pair of contacts (including, of course, a new spring arm). After dealing with the contacts as described, wipe away any metal dust with a petrol-dampened cloth and check the gap.

The Ignition Lever Cable. On the 1955–8 "Magdyno" models (19, ES2, 50) the ignition control is cable-operated by an ignition lever on the handlebars (*see* Figs. 1, 2). It is possible to make an adjustment of the cable by sliding the rubber shroud (*see* Fig. 29) up the cable outer casing and adjusting the hexagon screw thereby exposed.

If it is necessary to renew the control cable, unscrew the control barrel, draw the cable and plunger upwards as far as possible and slide the nipple sideways out of the hole in the plunger. Thread the new cable through the casing and solder the nipple to the end. Insert through appropriate

---

* Note that the latest type Lucas contacts have slightly convex (not flat) faces, which must be cleaned with fine emery cloth only.

parts, slide the nipple into the plunger, screw home the control barrel, adjust, and replace the rubber shroud.

The Slip-ring. Moisture, oil, or dirt accumulating on the "Magdyno" slip-ring is liable to cause difficult starting and misfiring. Very occasionally remove the h.t. pick-up from the "Magdyno" and thoroughly clean the flanges and track of the slip-ring. Do this by holding a soft, dry cloth, wrapped round a pencil, through the pick-up hole, and, with the cloth

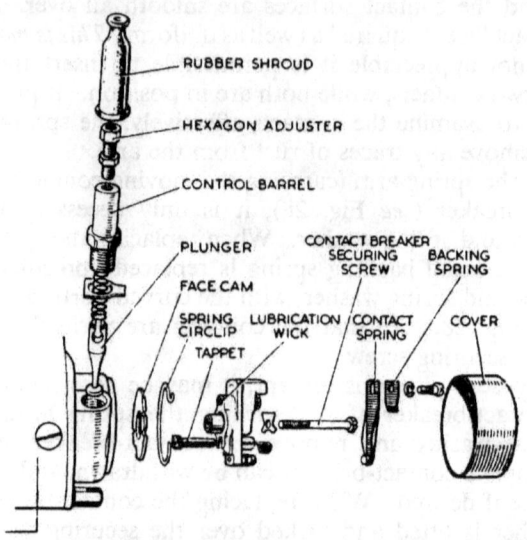

FIG. 29. THE CONTACT-BREAKER AND IGNITION CONTROL SHOWN DISMANTLED (1955–8)

lightly pressed against the slip-ring, slowly turn the engine. The h.t. pick-up is secured to the body of the "Magdyno" by two small screws which must be removed.

The H.T. Pick-up. When cleaning the slip-ring, also clean the surface of the pick-up moulding with a cloth moistened with petrol, and polish with a fine, dry cloth. Examine the pick-up moulding for cracks, and closely inspect the spring and carbon brush. The brush must move freely in its holder, but be careful not to stretch the spring. Renew the spring at once if it has weakened, and always renew a badly worn brush. When replacing the h.t. pick-up, do not forget to replace the small gasket between the body of the "Magdyno" and the pick-up moulding.

To Renew the H.T. Cable. The h.t. cable must be renewed if the rubber insulation has perished or shows cracks and becomes brittle. When renewing a cable, always use 7 mm p.v.c. or Neoprene ignition cable. Bare the end of the cable (*see* Fig. 30) for about ¼ in. and thread the cable through the moulded terminal nut. Pass the wire through the metal washer removed from the old cable and then bend back the cable strands as illustrated. Finally screw the moulded terminal nut into its terminal.

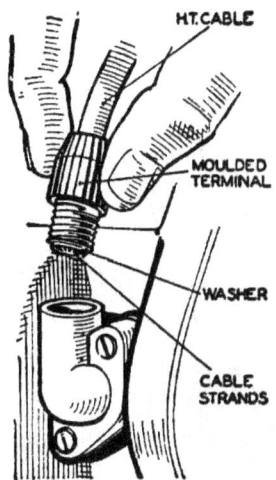

FIG. 30. RENEWING LUCAS H.T. CABLE (1955-58)

The "Magdyno" Chain. Lubrication is quite automatic, the chain being lubricated by the engine (*see* page 33). For chain tension, *see* page 80.

Removing Lucas "Magdyno" (1955-8). For instructions on removing the "Magdyno," *see* the appropropriate paragraph on page 80.

Removal of Ignition Lever. *See* page 81.

VALVE CLEARANCES

In order that the inlet and exhaust valves shall seat properly and have the correct degree of lift at normal running temperature, it is extremely important that the correct clearances should exist when the engine is *cold* between the valve stems and the rocker pads. The clearances should be checked now and again by feeling the push-rods. It is unlikely that adjustment will be needed, unless a big mileage has been completed, or the engine is new, or reconditioned, or the valves have been ground-in.

When Checking. Turn the engine over until compression is felt after the inlet valve has just closed, and then raise the exhaust-valve lifter a trifle, and further rotate the engine until the piston is at the top of its stroke and both valves are closed. See that the exhaust-valve lifter is in no way determining the clearance. There should be an appreciable interval between the moment when the lifter is raised and the exhaust valve is lifted off its seat.

Adjusting Push Rods (1955–6 Models). The correct valve clearances for 1955–6 models is *nil for both valves*. The adjustment is illustrated in Fig. 31. The necessary adjustments must be made with the engine *cold*, and it is important first to verify that the exhaust-valve lifter is quite clear of the exhaust valve when the piston is at T.D.C. on the compression stroke.

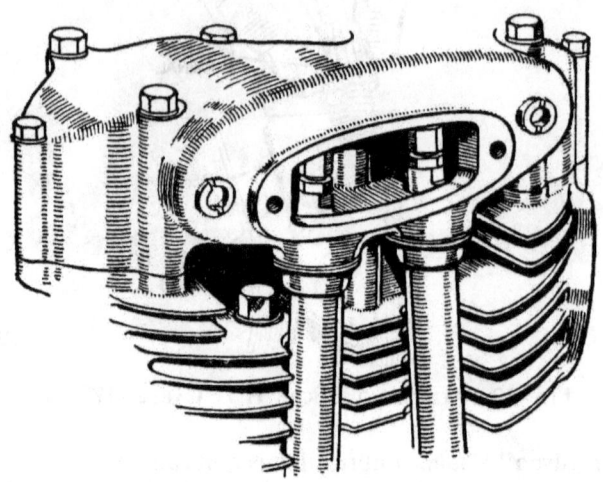

FIG. 31. PUSH-ROD ADJUSTMENT ON 1955–6 ENGINES

On 1955–6 engines a valve clearance of *nil* implies that the push-rods must be just free to rotate without any up-and-down movement when both valves are closed.

To make a valve clearance adjustment on a 1955–6 O.H.V. Norton engine, loosen the middle hexagon (lock-nut) by holding with one spanner the bottom flats on each push-rod, and applying a spanner to the middle hexagon. Then turn the top hexagon of the push-rod adjuster as required to obtain the correct valve clearance. Tighten the middle hexagon (lock-nut) and again check the clearance. Deal with both push-rods similarly.

Adjusting Push Rods (1957–62 Models). The correct valve clearances on Models 19, ES2, 50 are *nil* for both valves with the valves closed and the piston at T.D.C.

To adjust the push-rods, first check that the exhaust-valve lifter is quite clear of the exhaust valve when the piston is at T.D.C. and the engine cold. Then, referring to Fig. 32, release the middle hexagon (lock-nut) by placing one spanner on the bottom hexagon on the push-rod, and the second spanner on the lock-nut. Turn the top hexagon, the push-rod adjuster, in the necessary direction to obtain the correct valve clearance. Firmly tighten the lock-nut when the correct clearance is obtained, and again check the clearance.

Note that during the replacement of the inspection cover special care must be taken to avoid any over tightening. Over tightening can cause cover distortion, resulting in possible breakage or oil leakage.

Exhaust-valve Lifter Adjustment. As already mentioned, it is important that there should be some backlash at the exhaust-valve lifter lever, for it would inevitably prevent the exhaust valve from seating properly, and thus

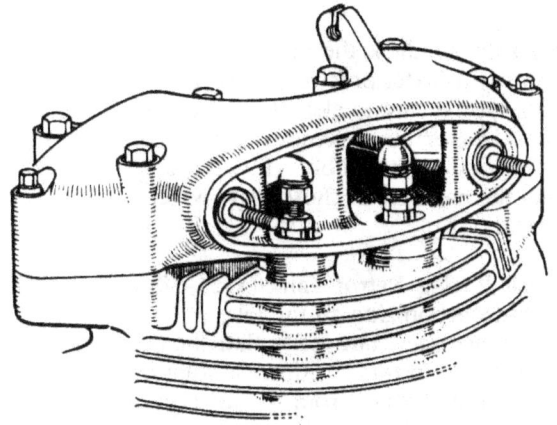

FIG. 32. PUSH-ROD ADJUSTMENT ON 1957–62 ENGINES

cause loss of compression and burning of the valve and its seating, accompanied by intermittent banging in the exhaust pipe and silencer.

There should be sufficient backlash in the control cable to ensure that the exhaust-valve lifter cam is always kept well clear of the rocker arm inside the rocker-box, when the valve lifter is not in use. The desired adjustment may be effected by means of the adjustable cable-stop placed on the near side of the rocker-box. If necessary, you can adjust the position of the operating arm to which the "business end" of the cable is attached.

DECARBONIZING ENGINE

After about 8,000 miles have been covered, the accumulation of carbon deposits on the piston crown and in various parts of the combustion chamber results in the engine losing its original "kick," and there is a marked decline in general all-round performance, accompanied by a tendency for knocking under the slightest provocation. In addition, the exhaust note becomes "woolly," and loses its virile crispness and low boom. When this happens it is a sure indication that the time has come for undertaking a "top overhaul," or, in other words, for decarbonizing and perhaps grinding-in the valves.

The Overhead-valve Engines. All Norton O.H.V. engines have detachable cylinder heads, and it is unnecessary to detach the cylinder barrel unless it is desired to remove the piston, to inspect it and also the piston rings. In order to remove the cylinder head, however, it is necessary first to remove the petrol tank, rocker-box, and push rods. On 1955-6 engines the head and rocker-box must be removed *together*. On later engines they must be removed separately.

Initial Preparations. Jack the machine upon its stand and get out the tool-kit. If the engine exterior is very dirty, go over it with a rag damped in paraffin, taking special care to clean the parts about to be dismantled, and see that a clean box or other receptacle is at hand in which to place the various parts prior to reassembly. Put the engine on compression and begin stripping the machine of those parts which obstruct easy removal of the cylinder head.

Removing and Fitting Petrol Tank (1955-58). Petrol tank removal is necessary when decarbonizing all models.

Draining is unnecessary, but verify that the petrol taps are both turned to the "Off" position. In this position the round end of each tap is pressed in. Disconnect the fuel pipes from the taps, gripping the union nut with one spanner and applying a second one to the tap union. To free the petrol tank from the frame on 1955-8 models, remove the four securing bolts and washers. Two steel washers and two rubber washers will be found at each tank support (*see* Fig. 33).

To replace the petrol tank, lay the four shouldered rubber washers on the frame tank brackets, and place the steel washers above them. Then position the petrol tank and fit the cupped steel and the rubber washers on to the tank securing bolts. The correct order of assembling the washers is clearly illustrated in Fig. 33. Next fit the bolts to the tank and tighten them evenly. Verify that the tank does not at any point foul the frame, and finally replace the petrol pipes, using two spanners as for dismantling.

Removing and Fitting Petrol Tank (1959). First make sure that the petrol tap is in the OFF position. Disconnect the petrol pipe, using two spanners. When doing this, hold the tap with one spanner while releasing the union nut with the other.

Remove the dualseat by removing the two wing nuts located centrally beneath the dualseat pan and lifting off the dualseat. This exposes the bolt which tensions the securing strap holding the tank down on the rubber pads taped to the top tubes of the frame. The removal of this bolt and bending back the strap enables the petrol tank to be lifted out of position.

The petrol tank should be refitted in the following manner: if new rubbers have been fitted to the frame top tubes, make certain that they are well bedded down and securely attached to prevent any possibility of metal to metal contact between the frame and petrol tank. Replace the petrol

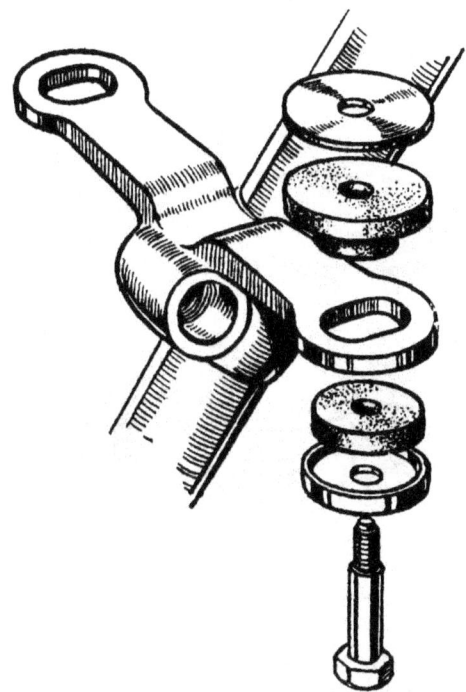

FIG. 33. CORRECT ORDER FOR ASSEMBLING FUEL TANK MOUNTING WASHERS (1955–8 MODELS)

tank and pull its securing strap into position. Fit the bolt and nut, and tighten sufficiently to prevent loosening by vibration. Be careful, however, not to over-tighten, as this may over-stress the tank structure. Refit the petrol pipe, using two spanners as used for removal.

Removing and Fitting Petrol Tank (1960–62). See that the petrol tap is in the OFF position and disconnect the petrol pipe. To do this, use two spanners if necessary. Hold the tap with one and release the union nut with the other.

Remove the dualseat by releasing the single Dzus fastener at the rear.

Then lift the dualseat and withdraw to the rear from the two pegs on the front of the frame. These pegs carry the dualseat by means of rubber bushes secured to its underside. Release the single rubber band securing the petrol tank at the rear and unscrew the two inverted bolts at the front. The inverted bolts have rubber washers above and below the lugs on the frame. The lower washers are in steel cups and the upper washers have a plain steel washer between them and the petrol tank. The inverted bolts are shouldered so that when fully tightened the rubber washers are not over compressed. Now lift the petrol tank clear of the motor-cycle.

Replace the petrol tank in the following manner. Check that the two

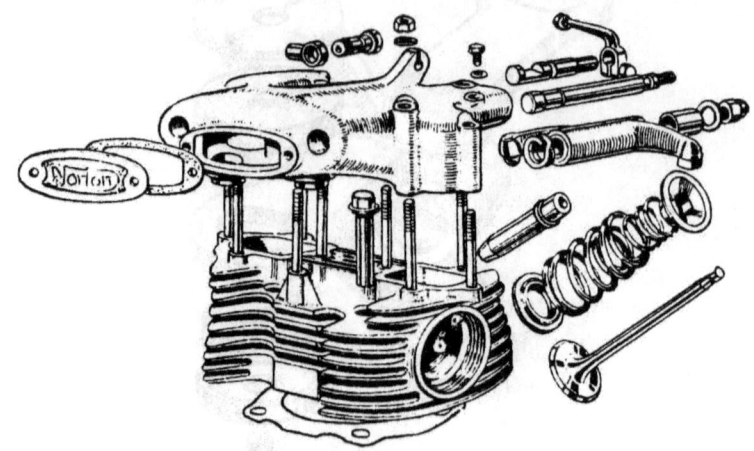

FIG. 34. CYLINDER HEAD AND ROCKER-BOX DETAILS ON O.H.V. ENGINES (1955–6)

rubber pads on which the petrol tanks rests at the rear (and which are taped to the frame tubes) are positioned such that the petrol tank does not make metallic contact with the frame. Replace the two bolts with their cups, rubbers, and washers at the front and pull the rubber band over the hook at the rear. Refit the petrol pipe. When doing this be careful not to over-tighten the union nut, as this may cause the tap to unscrew when the petrol pipe is next removed. Finally replace the dualseat and secure with the single Dzus fastener at the rear.

To Remove O.H.V. Rocker box, Cylinder Head and Barrel (1955–6). The dismantling procedure for decarbonizing a Model ES2, 19, or 50 is as follows. First remove the petrol tank as described on page 62. Then proceed to remove the rocker-box and cylinder head *together*.

Remove the two nuts securing the "monobloc" carburettor flange to the face on the light-alloy cylinder head, and withdraw the carburettor. The

GENERAL MAINTENANCE

air and throttle slides need not be withdrawn unless it is desired to dismantle the carburettor for cleaning (*see* page 48). With the "C" spanner in the tool-kit unscrew the exhaust-pipe finned locking-ring and remove the exhaust pipe or the complete exhaust system in one piece. Disconnect the oil-delivery pipe and the exhaust-valve lifter cable from the rocker-box.

Rotate the engine slowly until the piston is at T.D.C. with both valves closed, and disconnect the h.t. lead and remove the sparking plug. Now unscrew the four cylinder-head retaining nuts and, standing on the near side, lift the rocker-box and light-alloy head clear of the cylinder barrel spigot. When doing this, get someone to hold the two push-rods and cover-tubes. It is important not to mix up the push-rods, as they must be assembled in their original positions. Be careful not to lose the rubber and composition washers from the push-rod cover-tube ends.

Having removed the rocker-box and cylinder head together, separate them. Remove the nine nuts securing the rocker-box to the head and lift the rocker-box clear of the cylinder head studs.

If you with to remove the cylinder barrel (not necessary for decarbonizing) in order to inspect the piston and rings, turn the engine over slowly until the piston is at B.D.C. and lift the barrel off vertically. As the piston emerges, support it with one hand and cover up the crankcase mouth to prevent dirt or foreign bodies entering the crankcase.

To Remove O.H. Rocker-box, Cylinder Head and Barrel (1957–62). The correct procedure for dismantling for decarbonizing a Model 19, ES2, or 50 is as follows. First remove the petrol tank as previously described. Then proceed to remove the rocker-box and cylinder head *separately*. Unscrew the overhead rocker oil feed pipe top connexion from the centre of the near side of the rocker-box. Be careful not to lose the fibre or copper washer from either side of the banjo. Disconnect the exhaust-valve lifter cable from the valve lifter lever and completely release the nine-bolts holding the rocker-box to the cylinder head. Now remove the rocker-box from the cylinder head. Should it be necessary, break the joint by tapping the rocker-box with a light block of wood or with a mallet. Note that a thin composition washer is fitted between the rocker-box base and the top of the cylinder head. Be careful not to tear this washer during the removal of the rocker-box.

Withdraw the two push-rods which now protrude from the cylinder head. To remove the light-alloy cylinder head, first remove the exhaust system complete, loosen the air filter clip (where fitted) on the air intake of the Amal carburettor, and also remove the two nuts which secure the flange of the carburettor to the cylinder head. Now remove the air filter, followed by the Amal carburettor. Disconnect the h.t. lead from the sparking plug terminal. Then slacken all four cylinder head nuts and completely remove them. Note that a plain steel washer is fitted beneath each cylinder head retaining nut.

Lift the cylinder head off the cylinder barrel *from the timing side* of the engine, as this will bring with it the push-rod cover tubes which are held in

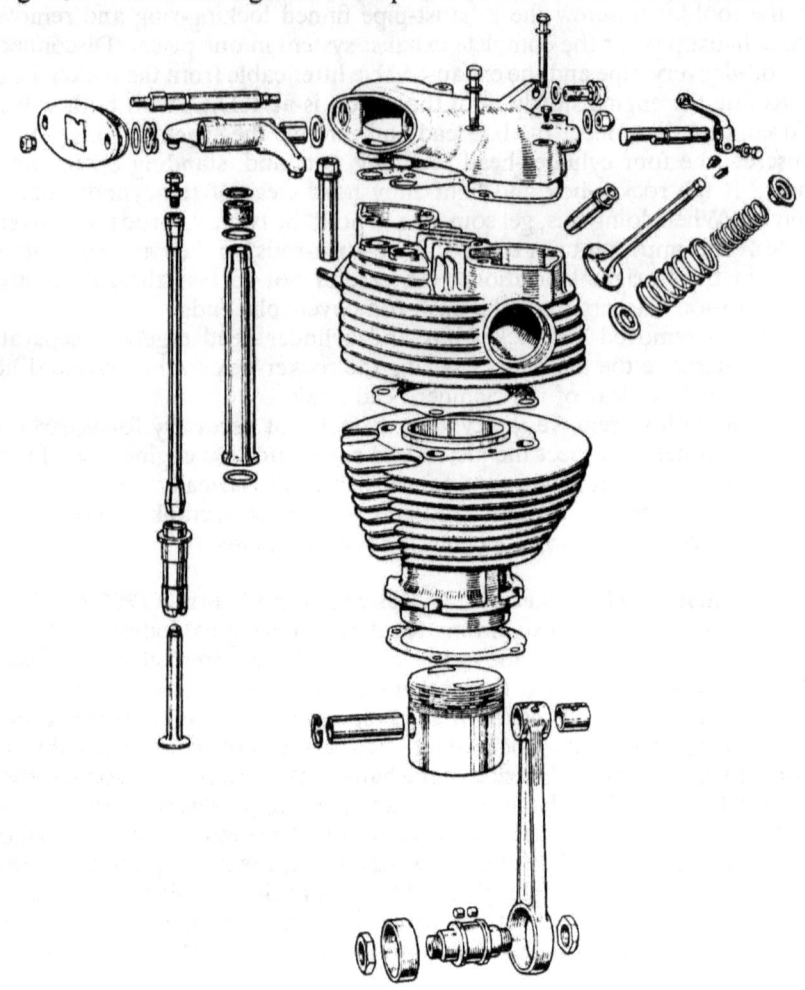

FIG. 35. EXPLODED VIEW SHOWING UPPER PART OF 1957–62 O.H.V. ENGINE
(Applies to Models 19, ES2, and 50.)

position by rubber sleeves. During cylinder head removal see that neither of the rubber rings comprising the cover-tube bottom seals is lost. Should difficulty be found in breaking the cylinder head joint, use a wooden block or mallet to assist matters. Tap the cylinder head *beneath the inlet port*.

Should you desire to remove the cylinder barrel from the crankcase (not necessary for decarbonizing), rotate the engine until the piston is at or near B.D.C. and gently lift off the cylinder barrel. As the piston emerges, support it with one hand and cover up the crackcase mouth with a clean cloth to prevent the ingress of foreign matter or dirt. All is now ready for decarbonizing, i.e., removing the carbon deposits.

Removing the Carbon with Cylinder Barrel in Position. Thoroughness in decarbonizing well repays the labour expended. To clean the cylinder head, the best tool is a blunt screwdriver, or a proprietary scraper, with which the carbon can be scraped and chipped from the cylinder head. See that the combustion chamber is not deeply scratched and do not forget that a *light-alloy head* is fitted.

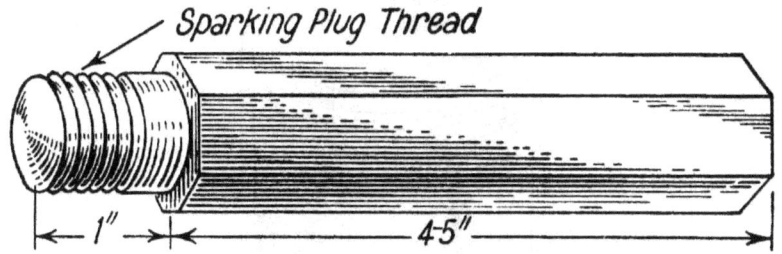

Fig. 36. A Hexagon Steel Bar Turned and Threaded at One End is Useful to Hold the Cylinder Head when Decarbonizing

Remove all traces of carbon from the interior surfaces and do not forget the sparking plug hole and the valve heads. Carbon forms less readily on a smooth surface. The ports, underside of the valve heads, and valve spring compartment cannot be cleaned until the valves are removed (*see* page 71).

In the case of the O.H.V. head, care should be taken that the ground joint of the head is not damaged. The method adopted at the works for holding the head while decarbonizing is to fit a hexagon steel bar screwed at one end into the sparking plug hole. The cylinder head may then be held in a vice by means of the steel bar. If such a bar (*see* Fig. 36) is not available, an old sparking plug makes a useful substitute. This will facilitate the operation considerably. Be careful not to damage the aluminium gasket.

With the comparatively soft aluminium-alloy piston be very careful when removing carbon deposits from the piston crown. On no account use emery cloth, but scrape off the deposits with a proprietary scraper or a blunt screwdriver. Avoid scratching the piston crown deeply, and afterwards wipe the surface with a rag moistened with paraffin or petrol.

It is advisable, before commencing to remove carbon deposits from the top of the piston, to place an old piston ring at the top of the effective bore and resting on the flat piston crown. This will prevent carbon being removed from the edge of the piston crown and the end of the barrel bore. When an engine has been in service for a considerable time, wear in the bore and the rings occurs, thus permitting a small amount of engine oil to pass. The carbon formed on the piston edge and the top of the bore acts as an oil seal. If this carbon is removed a temporary increase in oil consumption may occur.

Do not attempt to remove carbon from the skirt. Some carbon is usually deposited on the *inside of the piston*. If a piston is removed, this should be cleaned off. The screwdriver can be used for this till all carbon is scraped off ribs, etc., inside the piston. Take care not to let the screwdriver shank bump against the piston skirt, or the latter may crack.

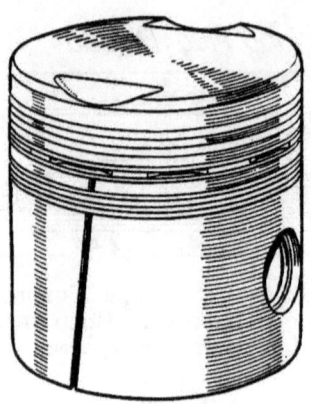

FIG. 37. THE FLAT-TOP WIRE-WOUND PISTON
By courtesy of " Motor Cycle," London)
Note the slotted oil-control ring.

Removal of the piston. As previously stated, piston removal is normally unnecessary for decarbonizing and removal should not be undertaken unless loss of compression indicates that the piston rings need inspection and possible removal.

The piston fitted to all 1955 and subsequent single-cylinder O.H.V. Nortons is of the flat-top wire wound type. On Models 19, ES2, and 50 it gives a compression ratio of 6·4, 7·1, and 7·3 respectively. Two compression rings and one oil control scraper ring are fitted. Holes in the oil control ring groove allow surplus oil to be returned to the inside of the piston. The scraper ring can be fitted either way up. As may be seen in Fig. 37, the piston crown has two grooves, fore and aft, to prevent the valves fouling the piston. The piston is of light alloy, and therefore great care must be taken to prevent its being scratched or damaged during or after removal.

To remove the piston after withdrawing the cylinder barrel (*see* pages 64 and 65), it is necessary to remove *one* of the two circlips which secure the fully floating gudgeon-pin in the piston. The gudgeon-pin circlips (*see* Fig. 38) are of stout design and their shape is such that only one end can be gripped with the Norton pliers.

The correct technique for removing a gudgeon-pin circup is to grip the turned-in end of the circlip with the pliers and then pull simultaneously *outwards and towards the centre*. Using this method, the circlip should leave the annular groove in the piston boss readily. It is important when removing a circlip in the above manner to *hold the piston firmly* with one hand so as to prevent any side strain being imposed on the connecting-rod, also to block up the crankcase mouth. A circlip falling inside the crankcase may cause horrible trouble. As soon as you remove a circlip, scrap it. A new one *must* always be used on assembly.

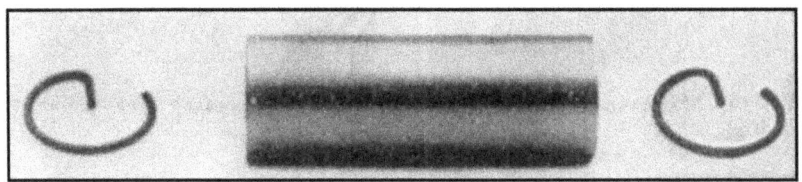

FIG. 38. SHOWING GUDGEON-PIN REMOVED FROM PISTON, AND THE TWO CIRCLIPS

Having removed the circlip, push out the fully floating gudgeon-pin. It is a running fit in both reamed piston bosses and the small-end bearing of the connecting-rod. It is essential to replace the piston in its original position. Therefore mark it on the inside in a suitable manner (*see* Fig. 39) so as to ensure its correct replacement.

Examining and Removing Piston Rings. The piston rings are the mainguard of the compression. They must, therefore, be full of spring, free in their grooves, and set with their slots opposite to each other (i.e. at 120° in the case of the three-ring piston which is fitted on all 1955 and later engines). If all three rings are bright all the way round, they are obviously being polished against the cylinder walls, and are perfect, and should be left alone. If, on the other hand, they are dull or strained at some points, they are not in proper contact with the walls of the cylinder. Perhaps they are stuck in their grooves with burnt oil, and will function properly if the grooves are cleaned. If vertically loose in their grooves or very badly marked, the rings must be renewed. Piston rings are of cast-iron and, being of very small section, must be handled very, very carefully. If not, they will certainly be broken. They cannot safely be opened out wider than will allow them to slip over the crown of the piston. Therefore, to put them on or remove them requires the insertion of small strips of metal,

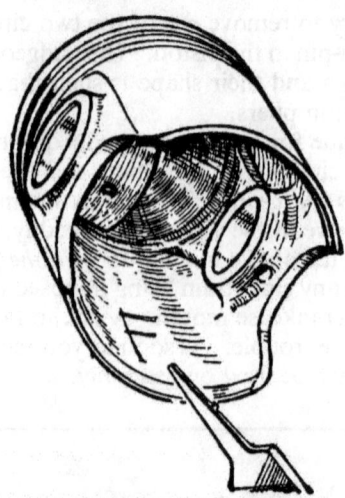

Fig. 39. Marking Inside of Piston to Ensure Correct Replacement
(*By courtesy of "Motor-Cycle," London*)

about ½ in. wide by 2 in. long, which are placed in the manner illustrated by Fig. 40. Be most careful to note the order in which the rings are removed so as to ensure proper replacement.

When fitting any *new* rings, thoroughly clean the grooves into which they fit, as any deposit left at the back will force new rings out and make them too tight a fit. Paraffin usually loosens stuck piston rings. Piston

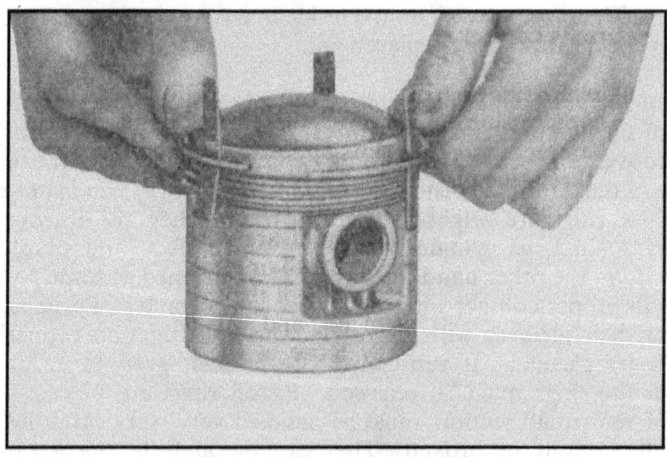

Fig. 40. A Safe Method of Removing and Fitting Piston Rings

GENERAL MAINTENANCE

rings are made to very accurate dimensions, and it is very bad practice to attempt to "fit" oversize or undersize rings unless you know exactly what you are doing. Lapping-in oversize piston rings is a skilful job, and unless the slot sizes are exactly right, the rings will not function well, and may even produce an engine "seizure." Therefore, always use piston rings supplied by Norton Motors Ltd.

Note that if it is decided *not* to fit new piston rings, do not remove the carbon from the backs of the rings or the bottom of the ring grooves.

If new rings *are* to be fitted, thoroughly clean the piston ring grooves. An ideal tool for doing this is a broken hack-saw blade. When the grooves

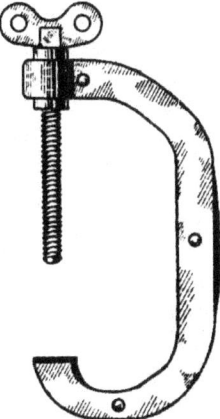

FIG. 41. A USEFUL VALVE SPRING COMPRESSOR

have been cleaned, check the new rings for side clearance in the grooves. This should be 0·002 in. Check each piston ring in the cylinder bore for the correct width of the gap. Place the ring concerned in the bore, push the ring down the bore, using the piston as a guide. Check the ring gap with a feeler gauge. With a compression ring the gap should be 0·010–0·012 in. With a scraper ring the gap should be 0·012 in. also. On pre-1960 engines, however, the compression and scraper ring gaps should be 0·012–0·016 in. and 0·005 in. respectively.

Removal of Valves (Overhead Type). This can be accomplished with the aid of a tool, such as the handy O.H.V. valve spring compressor shown in Fig. 41. To remove the split-type valve cotters on all O.H.V. engines place the spring compressor with the forked end resting on the valve spring outer cap, and the end of the screw in the centre of the valve. Then tighten the screw (and tap forked end) until the spring is compressed enough to enable the split cotters to be removed. The valve can then be drawn out and the springs and collars removed.

Grinding-in the Valves. Should the valve faces or seats show signs of serious pitting, the valves will have to be ground-in.* Do not grind them in whenever you decarbonize, as excessive grinding causes the valves to become "pocketed." About once every 10,000 miles should be sufficient if the valve clearances are correctly maintained. Valves of the overhead type have to be pulled up against their seatings with a hand vice, or pressed down with a suction tool.

Only grind-in a valve when necessary, using a proprietary *medium grade* valve grinding paste; only a small quantity is necessary, and do not revolve the valve round and round, but give a quarter turn backwards and forwards, frequently raising the valve from its seat and dropping it down in a different position.

The two valve stems may be cleaned but *they should not be polished*. Do not use coarse grinding compound for grinding-in. Some medium paste smeared very lightly over the valve face is far better. Richford's grinding paste is very suitable. Never continue grinding-in after a good seating has been obtained. All pitting should disappear and there should be a perfectly smooth matt ring round the face of the valve and the valve seating, indicating perfect contact. Depth of contact does not matter and about $\frac{1}{32}$ in. is quite sufficient.

After grinding-in the valves, be most careful to remove every trace of grinding paste. In the event of the pitting being very extensive and deep, it may be necessary to have the valves refaced and the seats recut by a Norton repair specialist or by the manufacturers.

Replacing the Valves. The inlet and exhaust valves must not be interchanged. Clean thoroughly the valve guides, the valve seats, and the valve ports. Also oil the valve stems which must be quite clean, but preferably not polished. Replace each valve and fit the duplex spring and collars. With the appropriate valve spring compressor (*see* page 71), compress the valve spring until the split collet can be inserted between the outer collar and the groove on the valve stem. Greasing the halves of the split collet will facilitate assembly.

The Valve Guides. After a very big mileage has been covered the wear of the valve guides may be such that the valves become a poor fit and irregular movement of the valve stems in their guides causes the valves to seat badly. In this case the valve guides should be renewed. The valve guides are a driving fit in the cylinder head and to remove a guide it is necessary to warm the cylinder head and tap out the guide with a double diameter drift. Use the drift to fit a new valve guide. After the guide has been fitted it is

* Always grind-in valves when renewing them, and before grinding-in valves which have seen much service, always check that the valve stems and guides are not excessively worn.

necessary to true up the valve seat with a cutter to ensure that the valve seat and valve guide are in true alignment. Note that oversize valve guides are obtainable if required.

Replacing Piston Rings and Piston. Fit the two compression rings and the oil-control ring to the piston, if these have been removed. It is advisable to oil the piston-ring grooves first and to fit the rings in the same manner as they were removed (*see* Fig. 40). The oil-control piston ring, shown in Fig. 37, must be fitted in the *bottom* groove and it can be replaced either way up.

Verify that the ring gaps are correct (*see* page 71) and then offer up the piston, with rings fitted, to the small-end of the connecting-rod. Make quite certain that the piston is fitted exactly in its original position. This is vitally important.

Oil the gudgeon-pin (Fig. 38) and insert this (in its original position) into the piston bosses and small-end bush of the connecting-rod. Push the gudgeon-pin right home against the circlip and then with a pair of Norton pliers fit the second *new* circlip. See that it beds down properly in its groove. Now all is ready for the cylinder barrel to be fitted.

To Replace O.H.V. Cylinder Barrel, Rocker-box, and Cylinder Head (1955-6). First arrange the piston rings so that the gaps of the rings are equally spaced (120 degrees). Next smear some clean engine oil on the piston rings, and cylinder bore. Turn the engine over until the piston is near T.D.C. Fit the paper washer to the mouth of the crankcase and see that it is undamaged and does not obstruct the oil hole for lubricating the rear of the cylinder. Apply jointing compound to both washer faces.

Place the cylinder barrel over the four long crankcase studs and as it reaches the piston, ease the rings carefully into the cylinder mouth. Gently slide the barrel right home.

After sliding the barrel home over the long crankcase studs, carefully clean the top face of the cylinder head and the bottom face of the rocker-box. Smear some jointing compound on both faces, but avoid using an excessive amount. Position the four sleeve-nuts which retain the cylinder barrel and head, and carefully fit the rocker-box (Fig. 34) over the cylinder head studs, and press the box home. Fit all nine nuts and washers securing the rocker-box, but preferably defer final tightening down of these nuts until the cylinder head and rocker-box have been assembled to the cylinder barrel.

Clean the bottom face of the light-alloy cylinder head and the top face of the cylinder barrel. Also fit the aluminium gasket (*see* Fig. 34) to the cylinder barrel face. Then offer up the assembled cylinder head and rocker-box to the cylinder barrel. When doing this get an assistant to hold the inlet and exhaust push-rods and cover-tubes in position, and to engage the upper and lower ends of the push-rods with the ball ends of the overhead rockers and the tappet cups respectively. Make sure that the inlet and exhaust push-rods are not interchanged; see that the rubber washers are fitted to the lower ends of the push-rod cover-tubes, and the composition washers to the upper ends of the cover-tubes. Now thread the cylinder barrel and head retaining nuts on the four crankcase studs and tighten these nuts down firmly and evenly (using a diagonal order).

Reconnect the oil-delivery pipe and the exhaust-valve lifter cable to the rocker-box. Adjust the cable adjuster as described on page 61 to give the requisite clearance between the rocker arm and the cam. Check the valve clearances (*see* page 59) and, if necessary, adjust the upper ends of the rods until the clearance is nil but the rods can freely rotate. Fit the rocker-box end cover.

Final Reassembly (1955-6). Replace the exhaust pipe, or complete exhaust system if this has been removed. With the "C" spanner in the tool kit screw the ring nut firmly into the threaded end of the exhaust port. Replace the Amal carburettor. Tighten the two nuts securing the "Monobloc" carburettor flange securely so as to prevent any air leaks.

Replace the petrol tank. Instructions for doing this are given on page 62. Note especially the correct assembly order for the mounting washers (shown in Fig. 33). Finally to complete the assembly, reconnect the petrol pipes to the float chamber of the carburettor. After a short mileage, check over the various nuts and bolts for tightness, and apply the appropriate spanners where necessary.

To Replace O.H.V. Cylinder Barrel, Cylinder Head, and Rocker-box (1957 Onwards). Position the three piston rings so that they are equally spaced. Also lubricate the piston rings, the bore of the cylinder barrel, and the piston. Next rotate the engine until the piston is near T.D.C. Fit the paper washer (*see* Fig. 35). When doing this it is extremely important to make sure that the cylinder oil feed and drain holes are not obstructed. Carefully fit the cylinder barrel over the piston and slide it right home.

Clean the cylinder head joint face and the top face of the cylinder barrel. Also replace the aluminium gasket in the position it previously occupied on top of the cylinder barrel. Replace the cylinder head (minus the rocker-box), making sure that the lower ends of the push-rod cover tubes are seating correctly between the tappet guide collars and the flanges on the bottom of the push-rod cover tubes.

Referring to Fig. 42, should the push-rod cover tubes have been removed from the light-alloy cylinder head, replace them with their components correctly assembled. The flat steel washer must be replaced in the bottom of the enlarged push-rod tunnel and held in place by the rubber sleeve. The angled steel washer must be placed over the reduced end of the push-rod cover tube before pushing the cover tube home into the cylinder head. To facilitate reassembly, smear with a little oil. Replace the cylinder head

GENERAL MAINTENANCE 75

securing nuts and lightly tighten each nut. Afterwards tighten firmly diagonal pairs of nuts. Having done this, replace both push-rods.

The next job is to replace the rocker-box. Clean thoroughly the joint faces of the cylinder head and the rocker-box. Smear the top face of the cylinder head with some oil and replace the paper washer. Now fit the rocker-box after inserting a bolt in the rearmost rocker-box hole. Replace

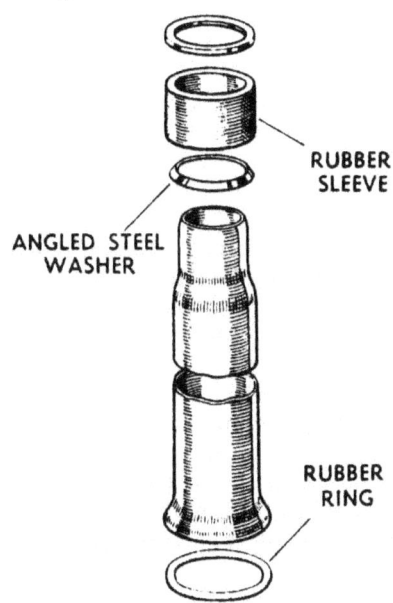

FIG. 42. THE CORRECT ASSEMBLY OF PUSH-ROD COVER TUBE COMPONENTS

and tighten lightly all nine rocker-box securing bolts. Afterwards tighten them firmly and evenly.

Finally replace the remaining components which were previously removed. Replace the sparking plug, the Amal "Monobloc" carburettor, and the air filter (where fitted). Connect up the h.t. lead to the plug and reconnect the oil delivery pipe and the exhaust-valve lifter cable to the rocker-box. See that the exhaust-valve lifter cable is correctly adjusted (*see* page 61). Remove the rocker-box inspection cover and adjust the push-rods (*see* page 60) to ensure that the valve clearances are correct, i.e., no clearance but the push-rods free to rotate.

IGNITION AND VALVE TIMING

Ignition Timing. Exact ignition timing is extremely important. For all normal road uses, the spark settings given subsequently (*see* page 77) should be closely adhered to.

It should always be remembered that should the timing be so far advanced that maximum explosion pressures are reached with the crank in true T.D.C. position, the big-end comes in for a terrific hammering for which it is not designed.

Retiming the Lucas "Magdyno" (1955–8 Models). If for any purpose the timing has been disturbed, it will be necessary to retime it, and to do this proceed as follows.

It is assumed that the Lucas "Magdyno" has been replaced on its mounting (*see* page 80), but that the driving chain and the "Magdyno" and inlet-camshaft sprockets have not yet been fitted. Replace the two sprockets and the driving chain. Tap the inlet-camshaft sprocket home (*see* Fig. 45) on the taper and key. After tapping the sprocket home, tighten its securing nut firmly. Fit the nut securing the "Magdyno" sprocket, but keep the sprocket free on the taper and do not tighten the nut. Next engage top gear and move the ignition lever on the handlebars so that it is in the *fully advanced* position. Then slowly turn the engine with the rear wheel until the piston is exactly at top-dead-centre (T.D.C.) on the compression stroke, with both valves closed, as described below.

Remove the sparking plug (O.H.V. engines) and insert a thin rod or thick piece of wire through the plug hole. By slightly turning the engine backwards and forwards you can find the true T.D.C. position where no piston movement occurs. Scratch a mark on the rod or wire (if a wire is used, see that it does not bend) to indicate the T.D.C. position and then scratch another mark $\frac{11}{16}$ in. (or whatever the exact ignition advance is) *above* the first mark.

Rotate the engine very slowly *backwards* until the top mark occupies and just passes the position previously occupied by the bottom mark. Now turn the engine slowly *forward* until the top mark exactly occupies this position. The piston obviously has now descended a distance equivalent to the ignition advance ($\frac{11}{16}$ in. or whatever it is), with chain backlash removed (by turning the engine forward).

If the cylinder head is removed for decarbonizing, the ignition setting can be accurately set by laying a small plate or a straight-edge across the top face of the cylinder barrel and taking vertical measurements between the plate or straight-edge, and the piston crown, using a steel rule.

Without moving the piston, now set the contact-breaker so that its contacts are just beginning to open with the ignition lever fully advanced. To find the exact point when the contacts commence to open, place a *very* thin feeler gauge or a *very* thin piece of paper between the contacts so that the gauge or paper is gripped, and then cautiously turn the "Magdyno" armature *clockwise* (contact-breaker side) until the gauge or paper is just freed on exerting a gentle pull.

With the contacts at the point of "break," secure the "Magdyno" sprocket on the tapered shaft. To do this, hold a piece of tube over the shaft and against the sprocket, and then carefully tap the tube. This will force the sprocket *squarely* home on to the taper.* Now tighten the "Magdyno" sprocket securing-nut with the appropriate box spanner. When tightening the nut, do not hold the contact-breaker, or it may be damaged.

After checking, and if necessary adjusting, the ignition timing, set the gap between the contacts (*see* page 55), replace the contact-breaker cover, retension the "Magdyno" driving-chain if necessary, and replace the "Magdyno" chain-case cover and sparking plug. Firmly tighten the three screws securing the "Magdyno" chain-case cover.

Ignition Advance (1955–8 "Magdyno" Models). On the O.H.V. Model, ES2 the correct ignition timing is $\frac{5}{8}$ in. before T.D.C. on full advance. On Models 19, and 50 the correct ignition timing is $\frac{11}{16}$ in. before T.D.C. with the ignition lever *fully advanced*.

Retiming the Ignition (1959 Onwards). On the 1959-62 coil ignition Models 19, ES2 and 50 the contact-breaker unit in which is incorporated the automatic ignition advance mechanism (*see* Fig. 17) is chain driven from the inlet cam spindle, the sprocket being located on the tapered shaft and secured with a central screw. Before attempting to check or time the ignition, make sure that the driving chain is correctly adjusted. Having removed the chain cover, slacken the two "Allen" nuts and the hexagon nut which hold the distributor housing to the timing cover extension and move the housing on its studs until there is about $\frac{3}{16}$ in. whip in the chain. Tighten the three nuts.

With a suitable feeler gauge verify and if necessary adjust the gap between the contact points to 0·015 in. when the contacts are *wide open*. Turn the engine over slowly so that the piston is at T.D.C. with both valves closed. Slacken the contact-breaker sprocket screw and release the sprocket from its taper. It is necessary to lever it off gently or else use a suitable withdrawal tool.

The contact-breaker body should be located from its housing so that the coil wire terminal is at the 6 o'clock position which brings the oil hole in the spigot in line with the plug in the top of the housing; at the same time the elongated hole in the clamping plate should be locked centrally about the set pin in the housing. Slacken the clamping bolt and rotate as required to obtain these conditions. Never attempt to rotate the square nut on the clamping bolt.

Turn the engine *backward* until the piston is $\frac{17}{32}$ in. before T.D.C. in the case of 1959–62 Model ES2 and $\frac{15}{32}$ in. before T.D.C. in the case of Model 50. Now with a small screwdriver in the slot in the cam end (not its central

* To loosen a "Magdyno" driving sprocket, tap on its securing nut lightly. If this is not effective, use a proper extractor.

screw head) rotate the cam *clockwise* until the contacts are just breaking as indicated by pulling on a thin piece of cigarette paper gripped by the contacts.

Valve Timing. The original timing should *not* be interfered with. On all Norton engines the timing gears are appropriately marked on assembly to ensure correct reassembly of the camwheels. If the camwheels are always replaced in the correct positions relatively to the engine half-time

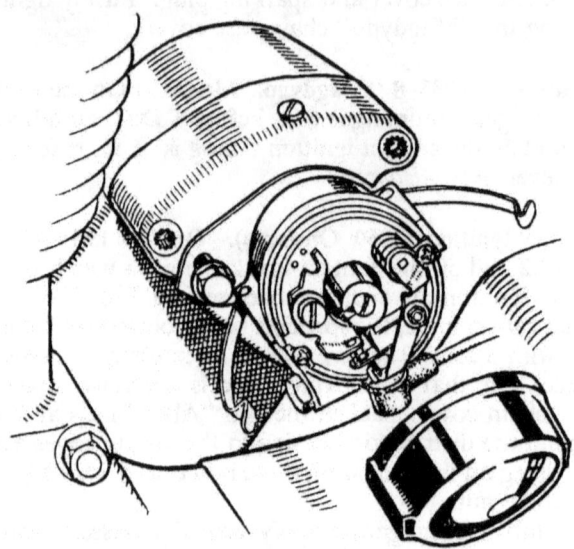

Fig. 43. The Assembled Contact-breaker Unit with Cover Removed

pinion (also marked), the valve timing *must* be permanently correct. In this section the removal and replacement of the timing-case cover are dealt with.

Removing "Magdyno" Chain and Engine Timing Cover (1955–58). First unscrew the three cheese-head screws and remove the "Magdyno" chain-case cover. Remove both sprockets with the chain in position. They are a taper fit, and the camwheel sprocket is keyed. If difficulty in removal is experienced, use a suitable withdrawal tool. Then remove the timing cover, which is secured by six cheese-headed screws* and two counter-sunk screws, the latter being in the "Magdyno" chain case. Having removed all

* It is important to note that the three top screws securing the timing cover are *shorter* than the three bottom ones.

screws, partly withdraw the timing cover so as to expose the timing gears and rockers. To prevent the inlet camwheel and the rocker coming adrift, hold them in place with a screwdriver while completely withdrawing the timing cover. When the timing cover is removed, the restriction jet for the big-end will leave its holder because of the spring pressure behind it. Finally, remove the spring (*see* Fig. 44) from its holder. Be careful not to lose any shims fitted to the camwheel spindles or the big-end feed jet.

Removing Engine Timing Cover (1959–62). First remove the chain cover which is held by three cheese-head screws. Remove both sprockets with

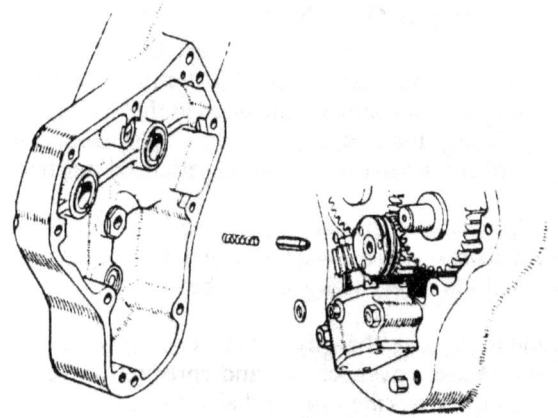

FIG. 44. DETAILS OF ENGINE TIMING-COVER
The "Magdyno" chain with chain case cover removed is shown in Fig. 45.

the chain in position. Should it be found difficult to remove the sprockets, use a withdrawal tool. A taper and key holds the cam spindle sprocket, but the contact-breaker shaft is not keyed. Remove the contact-breaker assembly by removing the set pin which holds the clamping plate to the contact-breaker housing, disconnecting the coil lead and withdrawing the contact-breaker. Alternatively disconnect the coil lead and remove the timing cover with the contact-breaker still in position.

Remove the engine timing cover screws and note that the three upper ones are shorter than the bottom ones. Inside the contact-breaker chain case will be found two hexagon-headed screws. When withdrawing the engine timing cover be careful not to lose the feed jet for the big-end. Also do not disturb any shims fitted to the cam spindles. Finally remove the big-end feed jet and the spring.

Replacing Timing Cover (1955–62). To replace the timing cover on O.H.V. engines, first clean the edges of the timing cover and timing chest.

Next smear the mating surfaces with some jointing compound or gold-size, and check the fibre washer on the oil pump nipple (*see* Fig. 44) between the oil pump and the timing cover. Offer up the timing cover and verify that when in position the fibre washer prevents the edge of the cover contacting the timing chest by $\frac{1}{32}$ in. ($\frac{1}{64}$ in. on 1960–2 models). This spacing is necessary to ensure an oil-tight joint when the timing cover is screwed home and the washer is compressed. Finally, fit the spring and the restriction jet in its holder, and evenly and firmly tighten all the timing-cover securing screws. Afterwards replace the "Magdyno" chain and chain case and re-time the magneto.

HINTS ON ENGINE OVERHAUL

After an engine has been in service for a *very* long period and it becomes somewhat "rough," a complete overhaul is desirable. Some useful general instructions on engine overhaul are included in this section. Those who are not very mechanically minded or have little spare time should have the engine overhauled by the makers or an experienced mechanic.

The Lucas "Magdyno." It is advisable after a very big mileage to return the complete instrument to a Lucas service depot for thorough inspection and overhaul, including regreasing of the bearings.

Removing and Replacing "Magdyno." It is necessary, first, to remove the "Magdyno" chain-case cover, chain, and sprockets cover. Then remove the h.t. lead from the sparking plug and also the dynamo leads. Referring to Fig. 45, remove the locking bolt *B* and the centre one of the three bolts *A*. Slacken the two outer bolts *A*. Now remove the Lucas "Magdyno." Replacement should be effected in the reverse order. Tightening of the bolts should be done *after* the chain cover has been replaced and the chain has been re-tensioned. Re-tensioning can be effected by moving the "Magdyno" in the required direction with the "Magdyno" security bolts slackened off. The total chain whip at the centre of the chain run should not exceed about $\frac{1}{4}$ in.

To Remove and Replace Dynamo. Removal of the dynamo from the "Magdyno" unit is dealt with on page 13.

Assembling and Dismantling Twist-grip. Grease that portion of the handlebars on which the grip operates. Referring to Fig. 45, fit the sleeve to the bar. Apply some grease to the drum on the sleeve. Then fit the spring and adjuster bolt and nut to the lower half-clip. Pass the control cable through the clip hole and fit the nipple to the drum on the sleeve. Assemble the upper half-clip and adjust the twist-grip for tightness by means of the adjusting screw, afterwards locking it in the desired position. To dismantle the twist-grip, proceed in the reverse order of assembling.

GENERAL MAINTENANCE 81

The Ignition and Air Control Levers. Both are of identical design (*see* Fig. 46). To detach the control cable from the ignition or air lever, open the lever fully, hold the cable casing, and then, while closing the lever, pull the cable casing from the lever body. You can now detach the cable nipple from the lever. After removing the external dome-shaped bolt, the various parts can be dismantled as shown (exploded view) in Fig. 46.

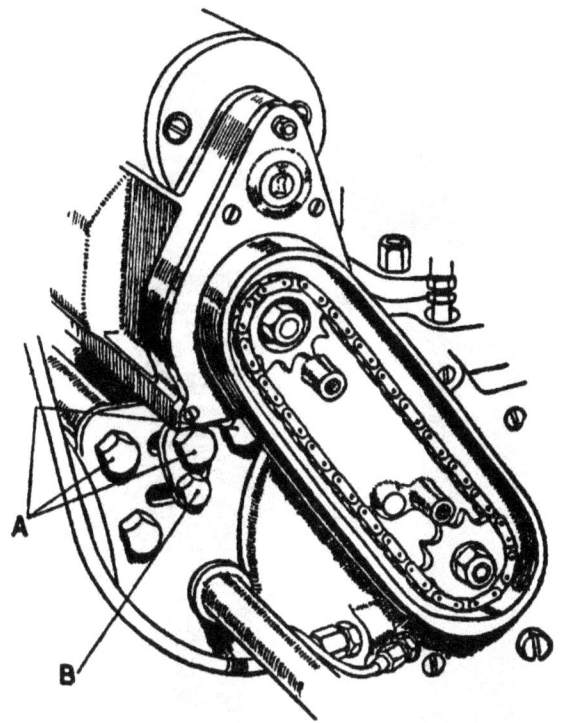

FIG. 45. SHOWING "MAGDYNO" SECURING BOLTS, CHAIN AND DRIVING SPROCKETS

When assembling the ignition or air lever, first grease both sides of the lever. To attach the cable, fit the nipple into the lever, close the lever, pull the cable casing away from the lever, and fit the cable to the lever body. Tighten the adjuster nut to give the correct degree of stiffness, and take up any slackness in the control cables.

The Exhaust-valve Lifter. To remove the control cable from the handlebar lever, turn the operating arm on the rocker-box by means other than pulling the cable, and detach the cable from the arm. Then detach the nipple from the handlebar lever and pass it through the large hole in the lever body. Be sure to fit the cable first to the handlebar lever when reassembling.

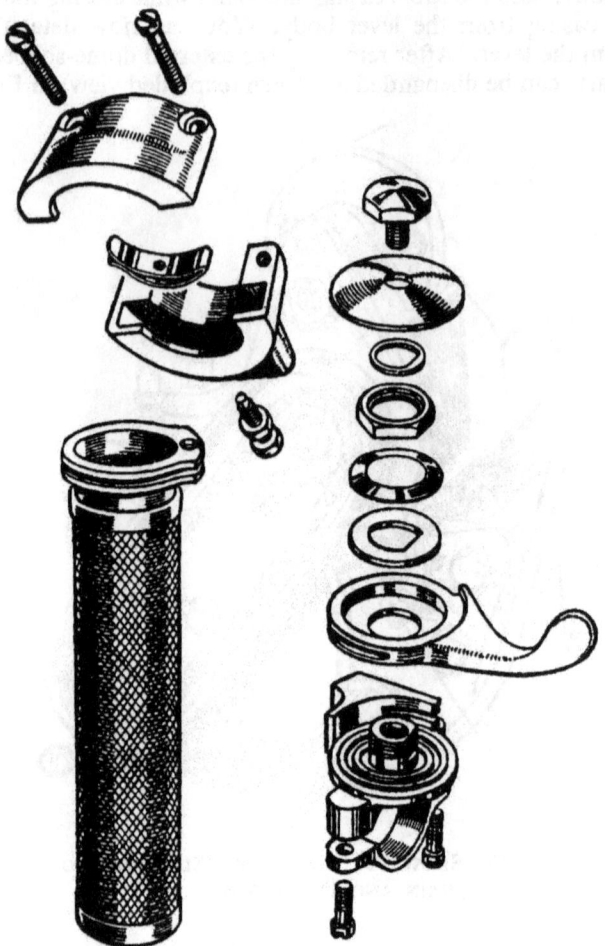

FIG. 46. COMPONENTS OF TWIST-GRIP AND AIR LEVER
The ignition lever assembly (1955-8) is the same as for the air lever.

Inspecting and Fitting Oil Pump. Unless absolutely essential, it is not recommended that the oil pump be stripped. It is advisable, however, when the pump has been removed to test for play in the spindle by pushing and pulling the worm wheel. By rotating the spindle while covering the oil holes with the fingers, it should be possible to feel the suction effect of the pump if it is in reasonably good condition. While actuating the pump, it should also be possible to feel any obstruction caused by the presence of foreign matter. Clean the pump thoroughly with paraffin before replacing it in the timing case.

It is assumed that the driving worm and nut (L.H. thread) has been fitted next to the engine pinion. Before fitting the pump itself, thoroughly clean the face to which the pump is to be fitted, and also the back of the pump. If jointing compound is used, employ only a light film and be most careful not to block up the oil holes. Examine and fit the fibre washer (*see* Fig. 44) between the pump feed and the timing cover.

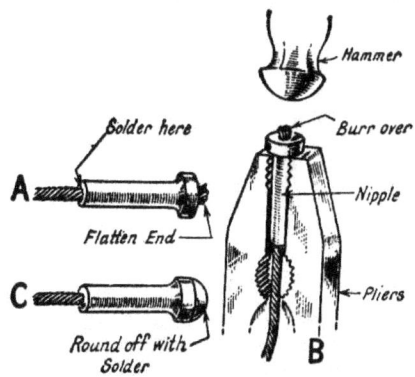

FIG. 47. How a Nipple Should be Soldered

Solder a nipple on to a control cable as shown in the order *A, B, C*.

Removing Timing Gears, Oil Pump, and Tappets (1955 Onwards). When the timing cover is removed as already described, the timing gears and the oil pump are exposed. Remove the nuts from the studs which retain the pump, and withdraw the pump unit (*see* Fig. 19). Next remove the oil pump driving-worm. This has a *left-hand thread*. Unscrew with a suitable key spanner or a hammer and blunt-ended punch.

Withdraw the two camwheels (*see* Fig. 48) and see that any shims fitted to the ends of the spindles are put aside for correct reassembly. To remove the small engine pinion, use a sprocket withdrawal tool.

Do not remove the tappets unless this is essential, as their removal involves the removal of the pressed-in tappet guides. These have to be extracted with a sprocket drawer. If the tappets are taken out, see that they are not interchanged.

The Oil Pressure Control Valve. As stated on page 34, the valve should not normally be interfered with. Should any adjustment be made, the adjuster screw should afterwards be locked. The usual method of doing this is to punch a little of the aluminium into the screwdriver slot in the grub-screw.

Replacing Tappets, Timing Gears, and Oil Pump (1955 Onwards). If new camwheels are fitted, it is necessary to check their end float and reshim if necessary. When fully home in the timing case the sides of the camwheels must clear the boss housing the pressure-release valve. Add such shims as are necessary.

Replace the timing cover and push and pull on the inlet camwheel spindle and then shim-up until it is just possible to feel the endfloat. In the case of the exhaust camwheel, the end float of the spindle can only be properly estimated when the crankcase halves are parted.

It is important to note that the inlet and exhaust tappets must be inserted

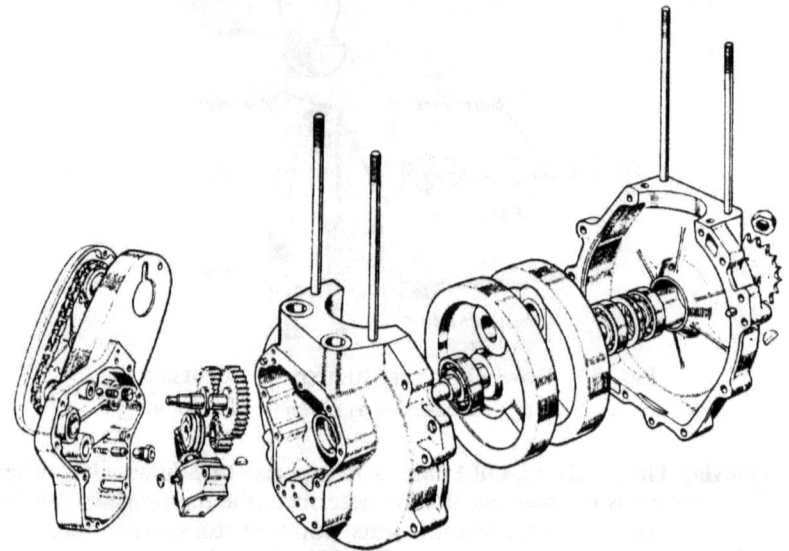

FIG. 48. EXPLODED VIEW OF LOWER PART OF ENGINE 1955-8

into their guides *before* the guides are pressed home by means of a tubular drift. A peg in the top face of the crankcase enters a hole in the tappet guide collar, thereby locating each guide radially. Before tapping or pressing a guide home, see that the peg and hole are in true alignment.

To assemble the timing gears, first fit the small engine pinion to the timing side main-shaft, and then turn the engine until the crankpin or piston is at T.D.C. Now replace the two camwheels (already shimmed-up). See that the markings on the camwheel teeth correspond with those on the teeth of the small engine pinion. Incorrect meshing will result in the valve timing being wrong.

Replace and tighten the oil pump worm with a peg spanner or suitable punch. The worm has a *left-hand thread*. Then replace the oil pump itself. See that the two faces are quite clean. Avoid using excessive jointing compound which might obstruct the oil holes. Examine and fit the fibre washer (Fig. 44) on the oil pump nipple, and finally replace the timing cover. Also retime the Lucas ignition.

Removal of Timing Gear Bushes. A close inspection of the timing-gear bushes may reveal wear which calls for the renewal of the bushes. The Norton Service Department is best qualified to tackle this job, and you should forward the timing cover and the corresponding crankcase half, or the complete crankcase, to Norton Motors Ltd.

Dismantling Rocker-box on O.H.V. Engines (1955 Onwards). The rocker-box of a Model 19, ES2, or 50 engine is fairly readily stripped

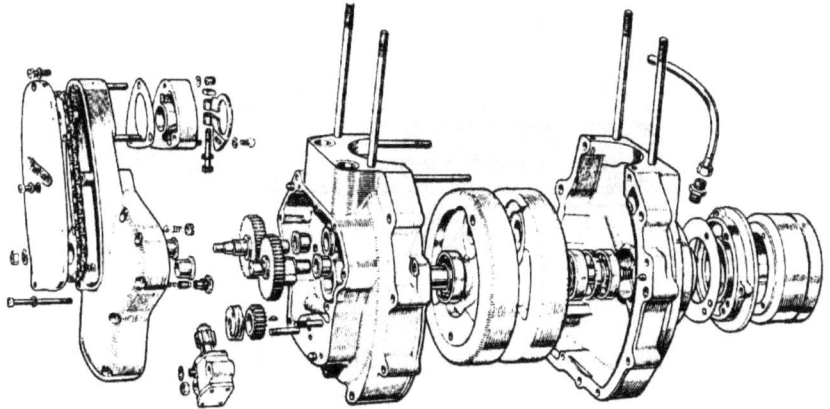

FIG. 49. EXPLODED VIEW OF LOWER PART OF ENGINE (1959-62)

down after it has been removed from the cylinder head. To remove the rockers for inspection and perhaps rebushing, take off the rocker-box inspection cover and remove the rocker spindle nuts and washers. Then drift the rocker spindles out by using a soft-nosed punch applied to their threaded ends. Afterwards extract the rockers from the rocker-box, together with their washers and shims.

To remove the exhaust-valve lifter from the rocker-box, first remove the small securing screw and then withdraw the valve lifter. The rocker bushes are a press fit in the rockers and may be pushed out as shown in Fig. 50. If renewal of the rocker ball-ends and pads is called for, drift these out from the rockers with a suitable punch.

Repairs to Rocker-box (1955 Onwards). If new rocker-ends are needed, press them into position. Make sure that the hole in the shank of the ball end registers with the oil hole drilled in the rocker arm. If new rocker bushes are required to be fitted, reverse the method of extraction indicated in Fig. 50. After pressing or drawing in new bushes, ream them both with a $\frac{9}{16}$ in. diameter reamer.

Assembling the Rockers (1955–6). The exploded view of the upper part of the O.H.V. engine shown in Fig. 34, indicates clearly the relative positions of the various parts comprising the rocker-box assembly. The steel shims on each side of the spring washer have the same Part No., but the thrust washer at the opposite end is considerably thicker.

To assemble each rocker in the rocker-box, obtain a steel bar of slightly smaller diameter than the large spindle hole and with a lead on one end.

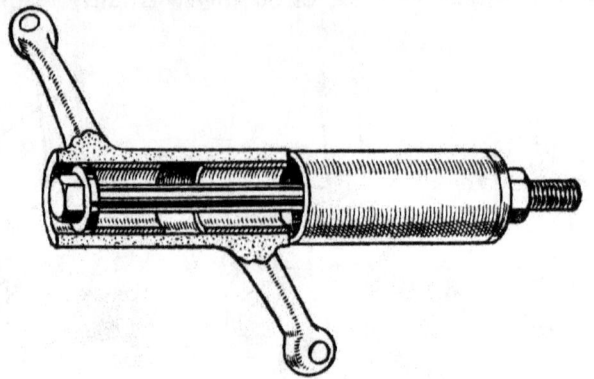

FIG. 50. EXTRACTING ROCKER BUSHES (1955 ONWARDS)

Slip this bar into the hole sufficiently far to enable the shims and spring washer to be placed over it. Now thread the rocker carefully into position. To ensure that the rocker goes fully home, it may be necessary to withdraw the bar slightly. Centralize the washers as far as is possible. Then remove the bar and insert the rocker spindle which should first be oiled. With a soft-nosed punch tap the rocker spindle so that it partially enters the rocker.

Next, with a screwdriver inserted into the push-rod hole (and bearing on the rocker arm), compress the spring washer, and position the thrust washer. Until the rocker spindle is tapped farther home the pressure exerted by the spring washer will retain the thrust washer in position. If the thrust washer is not truly aligned and is pinched between the shoulder on the rocker spindle and the rocker-box itself, tap the opposite end of the rocker spindle once only in order to release the thrust washer.

Again compress the spring washer by means of the screwdriver. This should enable the thrust washer to become properly located. Now interpose some tin strip or the end of a steel rule between the thrust washer and the rocker-box and tap the rocker spindle right home. Afterwards remove the strip or rule and verify that the rocker moves freely. Finally replace the copper washer and dome nut. Tighten the latter securely.

Assembling the Rockers (1957-9). The assembly of the overhead rockers in the rocker-box may need a little patience. The position of the various parts is clearly shown in Fig. 51. Note that a steel shim fits between the double spring washer and the aluminium spindle boss in the rocker-box, on the push-rod side, and the much thicker thrust washer fits at the valve side.

Obtain a tube or bar smaller than the large spindle hole on the push-rod

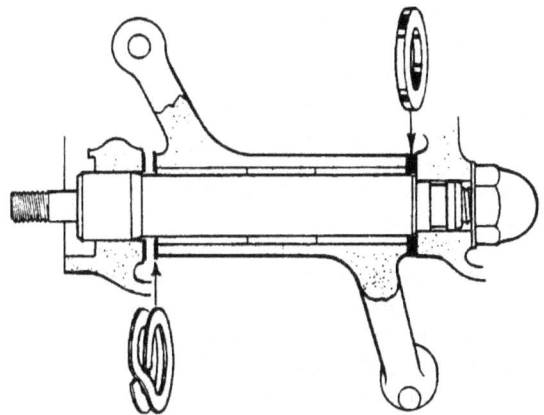

FIG. 51. SHOWING COMPONENTS OF EACH OVERHEAD ROCKER ASSEMBLY (1957-9 MODELS 19, ES2, AND 50)

side. Insert this far enough into the hole to permit the shim and spring washer to be placed over it. Position the rocker carefully over the end of the bar and push it approximately into position, and centralize the washers as near as possible. Remove the bar, smear the spindle with some oil, and insert the spindle from the push-rod side. Tap the spindle partly through the rocker, using a soft punch. Push the rocker over by hand to compress the spring washer and place the thrust washer in position. It will be held in position by the pressure of the spring washer until the spindle is knocked further home.

The washer is unlikely to be truly aligned with the spindle; it will therefore be pinched between the rocker-box and the shoulder on the spindle when the spindle is further tapped into position. Using hand pressure on the rocker, compress the spring washer again. This will permit the thrust washer to be positioned on the full diameter of the spindle. Now tap the spindle right home. Make sure that the rocker is free to move, fit the copper washer, and dome nut, and tighten the latter firmly.

Removing Engine from Cradle Frame (1955–8). Complete removal of the engine from the cradle frame, used on all 1955–8 Nortons, is advisable when undertaking a very thorough overhaul. This presents no great difficulty. First, remove the petrol tank (*see* page 62), take off the "Magdyno" (*see* page 80), and disconnect the exhaust-valve lifter cable. Then remove as a unit the Amal carburettor. If desired, this may be left attached to the control cables. With the "C" spanner provided in the tool kit, undo the locking ring which secures the exhaust pipe to the exhaust port. Remove completely the exhaust pipe and the silencer. By undoing the clip bolts and nuts, the exhaust pipe and silencer can be removed together, instead of separately.

Disconnect at the crankcase the delivery and return pipes leading to the oil tank. If the latter has not been drained, plug the end of the delivery pipe. Remove the oil-bath chain case, the engine sprocket, and also the clutch. Take off the front and rear engine plates, remove the engine cradle bolts, and lift the engine right out of the cradle frame.

Removing Engine from Cradle Frame (1959 Onwards). The engine and gearbox assembly is intended to be removed from the frame as a unit. Therefore it is advisable to support the frame on a box or block to provide rather more stability than is available from a central stand. First remove the petrol tank, the oil-bath chain case, the oil tank, and the battery, together with their platform. Also remove the engine steady-stay, and disconnect all cables and electric wiring likely to prevent the engine/gearbox assembly being removed when all the attachments are released.

Remove the remaining bolts which hold the engine/gearbox assembly to the frame and lift the assembly clear of the latter. To hold the cycle steady while removing the engine/gearbox unit, it is advisable to obtain assistance. Disconnecting the engine from the gearbox or vice versa should present no difficulty.

Inspecting Connecting-rod Bearings. Both the big-end and the small-end bearings can be inspected for wear when the cylinder barrel is taken off the engine. To examine the condition of the big-end bearing, turn the flywheels until the big-end is at T.D.C. Then grip the connecting-rod with *both* hands, and push and pull it in a vertical direction. Be careful not to exert any side pressure, as some end float is permissible. A small amount of up-and-down movement is acceptable, but appreciable "rock" indicates excessive wear, and a new crankpin bearing is called for. This necessitates parting the crankcase halves and the dismantling of the flywheel assembly. The former is a job which can be undertaken readily; but the latter, and the fitting of a new big-end bearing (and subsequent aligning of the flywheels), is a job best undertaken by the makers, who have the necessary jigs and tools available.

The complete flywheel assembly (or preferably the entire crankcase, stripped of parts not in need of attention) should be forwarded to the Service Department of Norton Motors, Ltd., or to an authorized Norton repairer. Those with some workshop facilities and experience can, however, tackle the job of renewing the small-end bush if this is found to be excessively worn. The gudgeon-pin itself is hard and is not likely to show much wear even after a very big mileage. It should be a good running fit in both the small-end bush and the piston bosses. Play can readily be detected by attempting to "rock" the pin in its bush. Obviously, if both the big-end

FIG. 52. THE STURDY BIG-END BEARING

and small-end bearings need attention, the whole of the work is best done by the makers, or expert mechanics.

Renewing Small-end Bush. To extract the worn bush from the small-end of the connecting rod, obtain a bolt about twice as long as the small-end bush. Fit a plain washer (with outside diameter less than that of the bush) to the head of the bolt. Then insert the bolt into the bush.

Fit over the screwed end of the bolt a piece of tube which has an inside diameter slightly greater than the outside diameter of the bush, and which is longer than the bush. Now fit a nut to the bolt, and to extract the bush, tighten the nut as required. Be careful not to strain the connecting-rod.

Prior to fitting a new small-end bush in the same manner, ream its inside diameter to the gudgeon-pin diameter. This is necessary because the bush contracts when pressed into the small-end, and it is desirable to avoid removing excessive metal when trueing up the hole with a reamer. Use an expanding reamer and ream in stages to size. Work from both sides and support the connecting-rod. Before finishing, drill the two oil holes in the bush. See also that the gudgeon-pin is a *running fit* in both the piston bosses and the small-end bush.

Splitting the Crankcase (1955 Onwards). First drain off all oil in the sump by removing the drain plug. Then remove the cylinder barrel, piston, timing gears, and oil pump. Remove the key from the driving-side mainshaft. Undo all the crankcase external nuts and tap out the bolts. Also remove the cheese-head screws from the oil sump. It is now possible to begin splitting the crankcase.

If the crankcase halves do not readily separate, some leverage is necessary. Turn the flywheels until the crankpin is near the mouth of the crankcase, and lever the timing-side half off by resting a lever against the crankpin nut and applying outward leverage.

To remove the driving-side half of the crankcase, lift the half of the case with the flywheels and lightly drop the end of the driving shaft on to a block of hard wood, when the crankcase half should part from the shaft. Considerable care is required when fitting the flywheel assembly to the crankcase and bolting the two halves together. For this reason the author advocates that when big-end trouble develops, the complete flywheel *and* crankcase assembly be sent to the Norton Service Department at Plumstead Road, Woolwich, London, S.E. 18 for their expert attention. If you have sufficient confidence, split the crankcase, forward the flywheel assembly only, and reassemble the crankcase yourself.

The Crankcase Bearings. These can be tapped out with suitable drifts, but the judicious application of heat to the bearing housings may in some instances be necessary. In view of the care required and the issues at stake, it is probably advisable for most Norton owners to entrust bearing renewal to Norton Motors Ltd. If the big-end requires renewal, the remaining bearings should be closely examined.

Assembling the Crankcase (1955 Onwards). Fit the flywheel assembly temporarily into the crankcase, and secure the crankcase halves by fitting and tightening *all* bolts. Then check the flywheels for correct end float (0·005 in.). If end float is found excessive, take out the flywheel assembly and fit pen-steel washers as required to both main shafts. To ensure central disposition of the flywheels in the crankcase, be sure to fit the same thickness of washers on each side. Replace the flywheel assembly, bolt up the crankcase, and again check the end float.

Next check that the connecting-rod is quite central in the crankcase, taking into account connecting-rod end float. Grip the base of the connecting-rod and push it towards the timing side as far as possible. Then measure the distance between the mouth of the crankcase and the end of the small-end bush on the timing side. Similarly push the connecting-rod hard over to the driving side and record the same measurement on this side. The difference between the two measurements should not exceed $\frac{1}{64}$ in. To make an adjustment for alignment, transfer pen-steel washers from one side to the other as required. After obtaining correct alignment, remove the flywheel assembly from the crankcase and proceed with the final assembly.

Oil the big-end and main-shaft bearings. Then smear some jointing compound or gold size on the two edges of the crankcase halves. Fit the flywheel assembly into the crankcase and bolt up the latter. Replace the timing gears and engine timing cover (*see* page 84).

Renewal of Timing Gear Bushes. During a thorough dismantling of the engine after a very big mileage it may be found that the timing gear bushes require renewal. The average Norton owner should *not* attempt this work. Dispatch the timing cover and half crankcase to the Norton Service Dept.

THE TRANSMISSION

Clutch Adjustment. Nothing is more exasperating or inconvenient on a motor-cycle than clutch-slip. The cable adjustment should be adjusted until there is approximately $\frac{1}{8}$ in. of idle movement at the end of the clutch-worm lever. It may be necessary to loosen the clutch-worm lever from the worm to find a more convenient operating position. The only parts of the clutch liable to wear are the friction plates, which are easily replaced. The clutch should be adjusted immediately any sign of slipping is felt, or if there is some "drag" present. The latter renders gear changing difficult, and the selection of neutral very uncertain.

When fitting up the control wire for the clutch, ease off the bends as much as possible to ensure long life and easy movement of the inner wire, and keep the cable greased where friction occurs.

To Adjust Clutch (1955–56). On machines with the Burman gearbox the procedure for taking up slack in the clutch cable is to loosen the lock-nut and then turn the adjuster for the cable as required. Should further cable adjustment be impossible or result in the clutch-worm lever assuming an unfavourable position, effect an adjustment by means of the worm lever. This lever is accessible on removing the two screws securing the oval cover to the gearbox outer cover. The oval cover is incidentally a good fit in the outer cover and on later models forms an outrigger bearing for the clutch-operating worm.

If the oval cover referred to above is tight, tap round it gently until the ends stand away from the outer cover and provide two lips into which suitable levers may be inserted. Be careful not to use excessive force.

To make a worm-lever adjustment, slacken the cable adjuster right down and then turn the lever on the shank of the worm after releasing the pinch bolt and while holding the shank by means of the slot machined across its end. Turn the clutch-worm lever *anti-clockwise* until it is about 45 degrees below the horizontal. Then effect the necessary cable adjustment and verify that the angle between the cable and worm lever is approximately a right-angle with the clutch fully disengaged. No adjustment of the clutch-spring pressure is provided, and the clutch-spring pins must be kept screwed fully home.

To Adjust Clutch (1957–9). Correct clutch adjustment on machines with the AMC gearbox should be obtained in the following manner. Screw down the cable adjuster as far as possible. Remove the outer portion of the oil-bath chain case (*see* page 96), release the nut locking the adjuster stud in the centre of the aluminium clutch pressure plate, and screw in the stud until contact with the long push-rod can be felt. Screw back *half a turn* and re-lock the nut. Readjust the cable adjuster until there is $\frac{1}{8}$ in. to $\frac{3}{16}$ in. idle movement before tension occurs in the cable.

Correct clutch adjustment is obtained when the adjusting screws are flush with the ends of the spring boxes and when individual adjustment has been made to ensure that the clutch pressure plate withdraws squarely as seen when the oil-bath cover is removed and the clutch lever is operated.

Clutch Adjustment (1960–62). The clutches of 1960–62 coil-ignition models have bonded on friction material and it is bonded to the driven plates instead of having inserts in the driving plates and chainwheel as on earlier models. Correct clutch adjustment should be effected as below.

With the clutch control cable slackened off, there should be about $\frac{1}{8}$ in. free movement in the small operating lever in the kick-starter case. This is shown in the extreme right of Fig. 53. If there is more or less than this, remove the outer half of the oil-bath chain case (*see* Fig. 56). Now release the locknut ($\frac{7}{16}$ in. Whit. hex.) on the adjuster screw in the centre of the aluminium pressure plate and set the screw as necessary. If it is first screwed in until it is hard on the push-rod and then slackened back half a turn, this should give about the right amount of free movement in the lever as described.

Tighten the lock-nut and adjust the cable so that there is about $\frac{1}{8}$ in. free movement at the handlebar lever. The clutch pressure plate should now come off squarely and rotate true laterally when the kick-starter is operated with the clutch withdrawn. Should it not do so, adjust individual springs to obtain this result.

If for any reason the clutch is dismantled, check that the nut securing the clutch centre to the gearbox mainshaft is tight before refitting the pressure plate and springs, etc. If a new handlebar lever is fitted at any time, see that it has the correct centres for cable nipple and fulcrum pin. These should be $\frac{7}{8}$ in.

Gearbox Lubrication. *See* page 35.

Primary Chain Adjustment (1955–6). The chain is automatically lubricated and enclosed in an oil-bath chain case; stretching takes considerably longer than is the case with the secondary chain, which is much more exposed to harmful influences. However, it will stretch in time, and it must be retensioned correctly. The chain should be adjusted and kept adjusted,

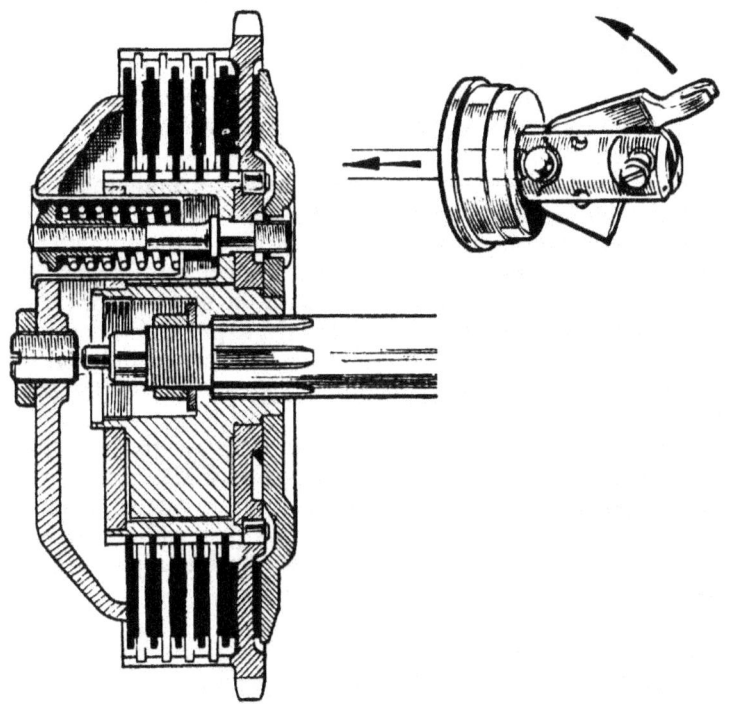

FIG. 53. SHOWING DETAILS OF LATEST NORTON CLUTCH
Prior to 1960 inserts were fitted on the driving plates.

so that it can be given midway by pressure with the fingers a total and maximum deflection* of roughly ½ in. Adjustment is effected by slackening the top and bottom Burman gearbox-bolts, and turning the adjuster on the offside of the machine clockwise until the correct tension is arrived at. Retighten the two gearbox bolts and retension the secondary chain.

Primary Chain Adjustment (1957 Onwards). The AMC gearbox pivots on its lower mounting bolt and elongated holes are provided in the mounting plates for the top bolt so that the gearbox can be moved backwards or forwards to adjust the tension of the primary chain. A drawbolt fitted to

* Always check the tension of a chain with the chain in various positions, and adjust with the chain in its tightest position.

the gearbox top bolt has a $\frac{7}{16}$ in. Whit. hexagon nut on either side of a stop rivetted to the off-side mounting plate.

To tighten the primary chain, remove the oil-bath chaincase inspection cover, slacken the forward drawbolt nut and run it back with the fingers one or two threads. Slacken the gearbox top bolt ($\frac{7}{16}$ in. Whit. hex.) and slacken only slightly the gearbox bottom bolt ($\frac{3}{8}$ in. Whit. hex.). With a spanner applied to the rearward drawbolt nut, pull the gearbox backward until the chain is tight. Now loosen the rearward nut a few turns and tighten the forward nut so that it pushes the gearbox forward until there is $\frac{1}{2}$ in. to $\frac{3}{4}$ in. up and down movement in the chain run midway between the two sprockets.

Tighten the top and bottom gearbox bolts and operate the kick-starter to check for the tightest point of chain tension. There should be a minimum up and down movement of $\frac{1}{2}$ in. In the case of the primary chain the tension is preferably *not excessively tight*. Tighten the forward drawbolt nut against the stop so that it tends to push the gearbox forward all the time, and tighten the rearward nut just enough to prevent its becoming lost. By doing this, backlash in the adjusting mechanism will all be taken up so as to hold the gearbox forward against the greater pull of the secondary chain.

Note that the pull of the secondary chain is always greater than that of the primary chain and can move the gearbox back after a jerky start or a very quick gear change, or if a pillion passenger is carried, if the tension of the secondary chain has been set excessively tight with the weight of the machine only on the wheels. In other words, any final adjusting movement should always be made in a *forward* direction.

Secondary Chain Adjustment (1955–6).

The chain requires to be tensioned at regular intervals, depending upon the mileage of the machine and how the rider has lubricated the chain (*see* page 36).

To retension the secondary chain, first on 1955 models unscrew the wing-nut (*E*, Fig. 54) on the rear-brake rod and slightly loosen the two hub-spindle nuts *A*.

On pre-1956 spring-frame models, after slackening the rear-brake adjuster nut and the hub-spindle nuts, adjust the tension of the chain in the following manner. Referring to Fig. 54, slacken the two drawbolt-adjuster lock-nuts *C* and with the appropriate spanner turn both drawbolt-adjuster nuts *B* clockwise *the same amount* until the total chain movement (with the chain in its tightest position) midway between the sprockets on the lower run is approximately $\frac{3}{4}$ in. *with the weight of the machine on the rear wheel.*

On 1956 spring-frame models unscrew the rear-brake adjuster nut, loosen both spindle nuts, slacken the adjuster screw lock-nuts, and turn the adjuster screws *anti-clockwise* the same amount until the chain tension is correct (*see* previous paragraph).

GENERAL MAINTENANCE

Tighten the two small lock-nuts and the hub-spindle nuts securely, and check that the wheel alignment has not been upset during the above chain adjustment (*see* page 112). Also readjust the rear brake (*see* page 109).

Secondary Chain Adjustment (1957 Onwards). Before commencing to re-tension the secondary chain, make sure that the primary chain is

FIG. 54. THE SECONDARY-CHAIN ADJUSTMENT ON SPRING FRAME NORTONS (1955)

On later models adjuster screws are used instead of drawbolts.

A. Hub-spindle nut
B. Drawbolt-adjuster nut
C. Drawbolt-adjuster lock-nut
D. Drawbolt
E. Brake-rod adjuster nut

correctly adjusted as previously described. Then proceed to adjust the secondary chain in the following manner.

First check that the ends of the rear wheel adjuster screws are hard up against the collars on the rear wheel spindle nuts. Next slacken the spindle nuts ($\frac{1}{2}$ in. Whit. hex.). Do not slacken fully but *about half a turn* so that the spindle will not move about too easily in the rear fork ends. Now slacken the adjuster screw lock-nuts ($\frac{3}{16}$ in. Whit. hex.) and count the number of flats you unscrew each adjuster ($\frac{1}{8}$ in. Whit.) so that you move the spindle back the same amount on each side, and thus maintain the wheels in true alignment.

With the rear shock absorbers compressed to mid-stroke there should be an up and down movement of $\frac{3}{4}$ in. to 1 in. in the run of the secondary chain midway between the sprockets. At this point the chain is at its tightest. If necessary obtain assistance to hold the shock absorbers down. It will help (if it is done single-handed) to set the shock absorbers to the softest position, and sit astride the rear number plate cuff, with the machine off its central stand. Be careful not to break the stop-tail lamp! Now check the tension of the secondary chain with the left hand. Check for the tightest point as described for the primary chain on page 94. Tighten the wheel spindle nuts and the adjuster lock-nuts, holding the adjusters with a second spanner if necessary to prevent them screwing in and thus away from the wheel spindle as the lock-nuts are tightened.

After adjusting the tension of the secondary chain, check the adjustment of the rear brake (*see* page 109) because movement of the rear wheel spindle alters the brake adjustment. Also check the alignment of the wheels (*see* page 112). This alignment is most important.

Some Hints About Chains. Never run them excessively tight. It is better to run them a little slack, provided that the chain does not make contact with the inside of the chain case or chain guard. Excessive slackness of a primary chain on some models causes an intermittent metallic tap as the lower run of the chain strikes the underside of the tube which surrounds the footrest hanger. There must always be enough oil in the oil-bath chain case for the lower run to dip in the oil.

Chain Stretch. A simple check for chain stretch is to remove the chain from the machine, lay it on a flat surface, and stretch it to its full extent. Measure 24 pitches between bearing-pin centres. In the event of the chain showing more than one-quarter of an inch per foot elongation, renew the chain.

The Spring Link. Always reconnect a chain so that the *closed* end of the spring link faces the direction of chain travel. This is most important.

To Remove Oil-bath Chain Case (1955–58). Remove the footrest rod, and the rear brake-pedal. Then remove the large nut which secures the outer portion of the oil-bath, and detach the latter. Next remove the clutch-spring screws, the clutch springs, and the cups. Each of these members is in triplicate. Also remove the clutch outer-plate, the clutch thrust-rod, and the clutch retaining-nut. While unscrewing this nut, depress the foot change until first gear is obtained and get assistance to hold the rear wheel. After removing the retaining nut, withdraw the clutch body; to do this a special tool is obtainable.

GENERAL MAINTENANCE

With a claw-type extractor, proceed to remove the engine sprocket. Having done this, remove together the engine sprocket, clutch, and primary chain. Finally remove the inner portion of the oil-bath, which is secured by two bolts and two nuts. The inner portion of the oil-bath is secured to the crankcase by a bolt, to the engine plate by a nut, to the secondary-chain guard by a bolt, and to the gearbox pivot-bolt by a nut.

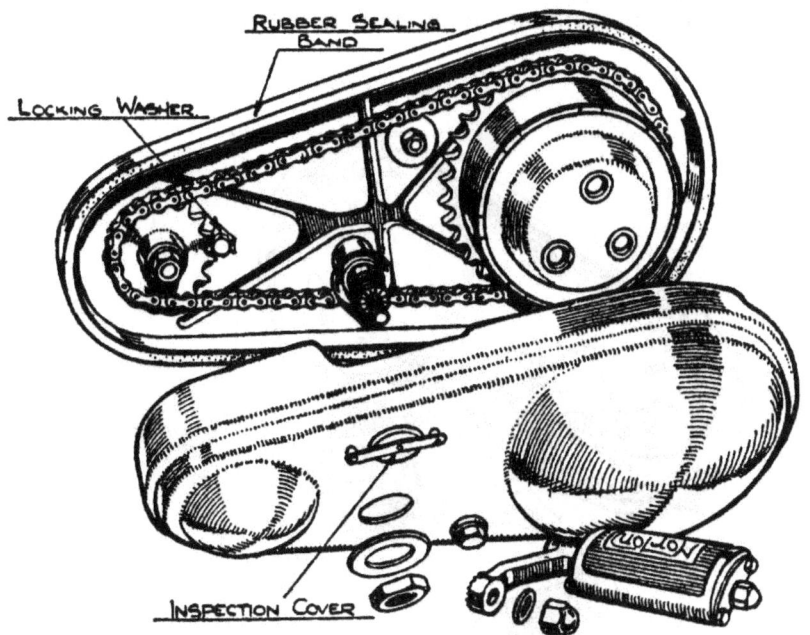

FIG. 55. OIL-BATH CHAIN CASE WITH COVER REMOVED
(1955–58 MODELS)

On 1957–58 models the clutch has an adjuster screw and lock-nut.

To Replace Oil-bath Chain Case (1955–58). Assemble it in the reverse order to that used for removal. Inspect the rubber washer fitted to the flange of the inner portion. This constitutes the oil seal, and must be in sound condition to prevent oil leakage. After assembly is completed, replenish the oil-bath with engine oil (*see* page 33) to the level of the plug situated close to the bottom of the outer portion of the oil-bath.

To Remove the Oil-bath Chain Case (1959 Onwards). Remove the rear brake pedal by withdrawing the jaw joint pin and unscrewing the grease nipple from the pedal boss. Be careful while doing this not to push the pedal down farther than it normally travels, otherwise the pedal return spring housed in the pedal boss will be strained and need renewal. Remove the near-side footrest and the large nut screwed on to the footrest tube (⅞ in. Whit. hex). This enables you to withdraw the outer cover exposing, as shown in Fig. 56, the driving chain, the clutch, and the A.C. generator. Remove the three nuts holding the stator and withdraw it from its studs, drawing the cable carefully through the grommet in the rear part of the chain case until the stator can be rested safely on the rear engine plates. Remove the mainshaft nut and the rotor from the mainshaft.

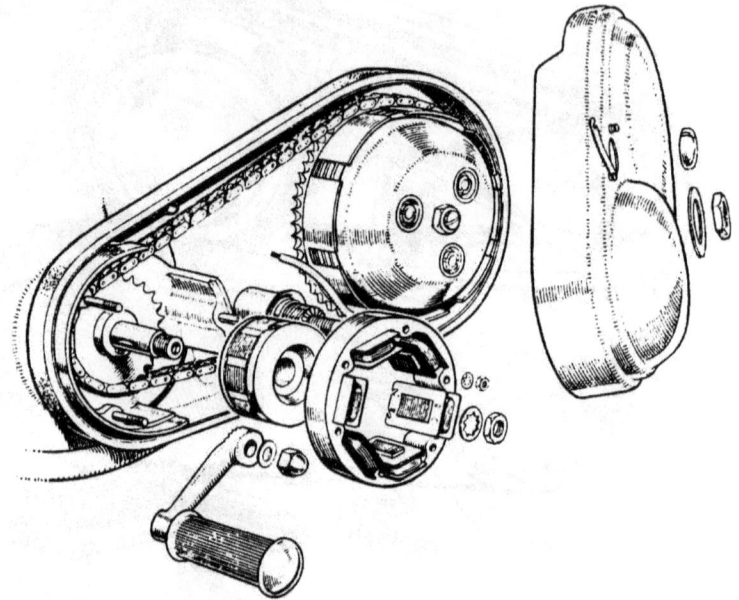

FIG. 56. OIL-BATH CHAIN CASE WITH COVER REMOVED (1959–62 MODELS)

Now remove the primary chain and withdraw the engine sprocket, using a sprocket extractor. Remove the three clutch spring nuts, springs and cups, and the clutch pressure plate. Engage top gear and obtain assistance to hold the rear wheel while the clutch retaining nut is being slackened. The rear brake can be held on with a ring spanner on the cam spindle nut.

Having removed the clutch centre nut, withdraw the clutch assembly; it is on a parallel spline, but if tight a special tool can be obtained from the Norton Service Dept. Remove the three countersunk "Allen" screws which secure the stator housing to the crankcase. The rear portion of the chaincase is now held by three screws at the front end, by the nut on the gear-box near side engine/gearbox plate. Note that a paper washer is fitted between the rear side of the chain case and the crankcase.

GENERAL MAINTENANCE

To Replace Oil-bath Chain Case (1959 Onwards). Reassemble the oil-bath chain case in the reverse order of dismantling. See that the slots in the stator housing are positioned correctly so as to pass the chain, and fit the chain spring link so that its *closed* end points in the direction of chain travel and with its convex side out. Do not fit the outer portion of the oil-bath chain case until the clutch has been adjusted if necessary (*see* page 92). Observe that the rubber sealing band has a thin lip on one edge only. This must be on the *outer* diameter of the band and towards the oil-bath chain case cover. If the band has stretched it is permissible to cut a piece out and join with wire, provided the joint is positioned on the top side of the chain case.

Fit the stator with the edge from which the leads are taken innermost, drawing surplus cable through to behind the inner portion. Replace the outer cover of the oil-bath chain case, giving the rim a few blows with the ball of the hand or a rubber mallet while tightening the nut. Avoid excessive tightening of this nut, otherwise some distortion of the case may occur. With the nut properly tightened only one or two threads should protrude through the nut.

Dismantling Clutch (1955–6). First remove the outer portion of the oil-bath. Also remove the clutch body with a special tool. If it is desired to inspect the driving slots in the clutch sprocket, it is necessary to remove the steel band which is pressed round the clutch sprocket. But if it is the rider's intention to dismantle the clutch plates only, it is permissible to leave this band in position. Its function, incidentally, is to prevent excessive oil getting on the plates.

To remove the clutch plates, detach the circlip (where fitted) which holds the plates on to the clutch body and withdraw the plates. It will be observed that they comprise plain steel plates, and steel plates with Ferodo inserts spaced alternate. Now remove the clutch sprocket.

Referring to Fig. 58, grip an old gearbox main-axle (if to hand) between the jaws of a vice, with the splined end above the jaws, and fit the clutch body to the axle. Remove all three screws holding the front cover-plate and tap the plate round until a screw driver can be used to prise it off (*see* Fig. 57). Now remove the clutch cover-plate and the shock-absorber rubbers (*see* Fig. 58). Remove the rubbers with a large "C" spanner. Place the spanner over the body so as to engage the splines as illustrated. Compress the large rubbers while removing the smaller ones. The length of the spanner should be such that the load can be taken by the operator's thighs, while both hands are free to remove the shock-absorber rubbers. A good substitute for a "C" spanner is an old plain steel clutch-plate with handle attached. To remove the large and smaller rubbers, it is advisable to use a small, sharp-pointed tool.

Remove the clutch body from the axle and replace in the reverse position. Then remove the three studs of the back-cover plate. Then separate the back plate, roller race, back cover, and clutch body.

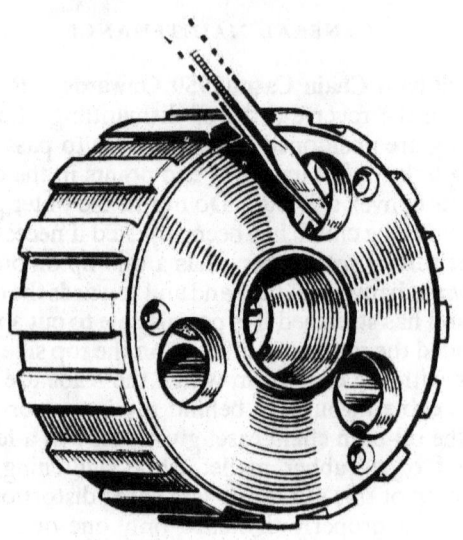

FIG. 57. OBTAINING ACCESS TO THE SHOCK-ABSORBER RUBBERS
The three screws are shown removed from the cover plate.

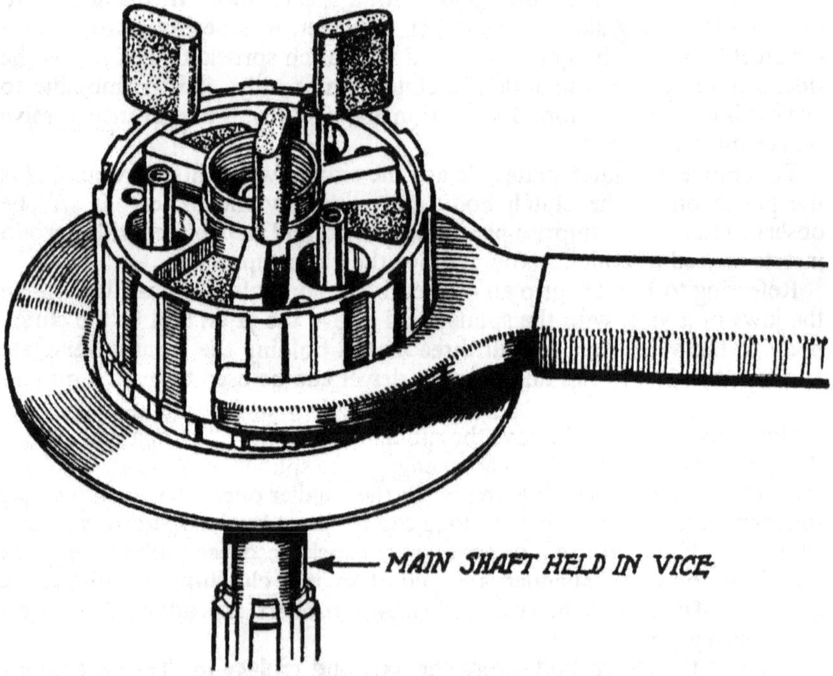

← MAIN SHAFT HELD IN VICE

FIG. 58. REMOVING SHOCK-ABSORBER RUBBERS FROM CLUTCH BODY

Inspecting Burman Clutch Parts (1955–6). When occasion is had to strip down the clutch (*see* Fig. 74), during a complete overhaul, make a close inspection of the various components. Visually inspect the inserts in each friction plate. They must be proud of the steel plate in which they are fitted. If new inserts are fitted, see that they are all level and flat, and all contact the adjacent plain steel-plates. The fitting of a few new inserts separately is bad practice.

Look for wear on the drive of the plates. The drive of the plain steel-plates is taken on the inside circumference, but that for the friction-insert plates is taken on the outside circumference.

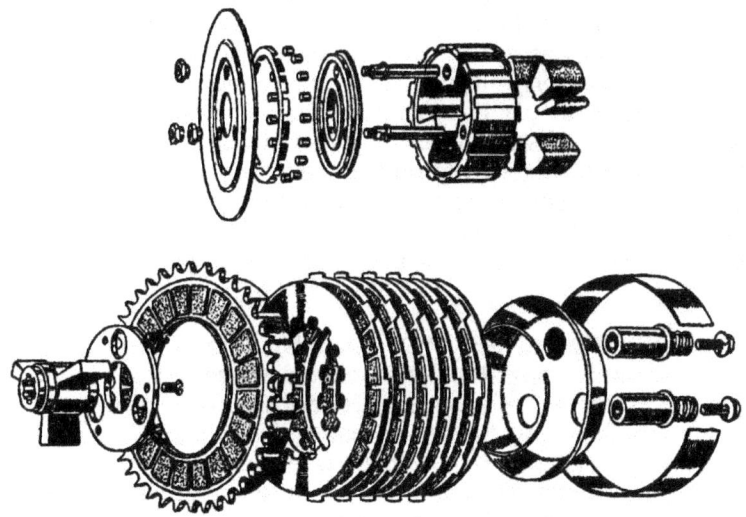

Fig. 59. Exploded View of Burman Multi-plate Clutch (1955–6)

The upper components should be regarded as being in line with and to the left of the lower members.

The splines on the clutch centre and the corresponding splines on the plain steel-plates seldom show signs of wear, but this does not necessarily apply to the tongues on the friction-insert plates. Sometimes these tongues wear, and occasionally they bite into the driven part of the combined sprocket and casing. Wear of this nature interferes with smooth clutch action. The remedy is to file or grind the tongues on the plates square, and also the edge of the driven part of the sprocket. The only ill effect will be some slight backlash in the control, which does not matter.

Inspect the plain steel-plates for signs of roughness, especially the back plate. Verify the condition of the bearing rollers, race, and cage. See if the back-cover plate is worn by the clutch centre. Also inspect the shock-absorber rubbers for evidence of cracking or softening.

Assembling Clutch (1955–6). Assemble the clutch body back coverplate to the body. Check that the mating holes are in alignment and the spring studs an easy fit. Replace the clutch-body centre and fit the large shock-absorber rubbers. Compress these and fit the smaller ones. Replace the clutch-body front cover and tighten the screws. Fit the roller race on to the back-cover plate, fit the clutch plate back, and replace the back-plate spring studs. Fit nuts to the studs and tighten them, finally locking the nuts with a centre-punch. Test the roller race for freeness on its track and apply a little anti-centrifuge grease.

Replace the steel band on the sprocket, making sure that the latter does not become distorted. Check all clutch plates for free movement and fit the clutch sprocket to the body. Rotate the sprocket on the race to verify free running. Next assemble the clutch plates on the sprocket and body. The correct order of fitting is: plain steel; inserts; plain, etc. The bevelled edges of the plates when present must be *towards* the sprocket. Turn the sprocket to see whether the plates are free.

Fit the plate retaining-circlip when provided and assemble the clutch to the gearbox main-shaft. Replace the clutch thrust-rod, clutch outer plate, spring cups, springs, and spring pins. Tighten the latter *fully*, and then complete the assembly by replacing the outer portion of the oil-bath (*see* page 97).

Dismantling AMC Clutch (1957 Onwards). First remove the oil-bath chain case cover (*see* page 97). Remove the clutch spring adjuster nuts with a divided screwdriver, or use a small screwdriver on one side only. Each screw has a locking "pip" under its head and considerable torque may be necessary to get over it during the first one or two revolutions. The clutch pressure plate can now be withdrawn. Remove the clutch plates and note that the first driven plate has bonded friction material on one side only, and must therefore always be the end plate. Disconnect the primary chain (*see* page 96) and remove the clutch chainwheel. Engage top gear and unscrew the clutch centre nut (R.H. thread) using a $\frac{7}{16}$ in. Whit. hexagon box spanner. Remove both the nut and the spring washer. Now withdraw the clutch centre from the gearbox splined mainshaft.

To dismantle the clutch shock-absorber rubbers, proceed as described on page 99 for the 1955–6 Burman clutch, noting Figs. 57 and 58. Then remove the body from the mainshaft, take out the "spider" or shock-absorber centre and turn the body upside down on the bench. Remove the three nuts on the spring studs and separate the back plate, the roller race, the race plate, and the clutch body.

Inspecting Clutch Parts (1957 Onwards). Examine the driven plates with their bonded strips of friction material and make sure that none are missing. Clean them thoroughly with a stiff brush and petrol. Place the driving plates together and check that they are flat. These should be of the "pin point planished" type, i.e. they should have small "pop" marks all over them. Plates so treated will not buckle at high temperatures. The splines on the clutch body and the bonded plates which drive the body rarely show any signs of wear, but the tongues on the plain driving plates may become worn and may have cut slots in the chain wheel. When the plates are operated this wear can obstruct the free movement of the plates. The remedy is to file or grind the tongues on the plates square, also the driving edge of the slots in the chain wheel. No ill effect of this occurs other than a slight amount of backlash when the clutch is disengaged or engaged.

Inspect the roller race, the rollers, and the cage. Examine the race plate, face, and bore for wear by the clutch body centre or "spider." Inspect the clutch shock-absorber rubbers for evidence of softening or cracking. Also look at the "spider" itself for signs of wear on the race plate and cover plate diameters. Examine the internal splines for any fractures.

Assembling Clutch (1957 Onwards). Fit the race plate to the clutch body, making sure that the holes in the plate are in line with the holes in the body, and that the spring studs are an easy fit. Fit the roller cage, the rollers, and the back plate. Replace the shock absorber centre or "spider" in the clutch body and lock up the nuts on the studs. Fit the large rubbers, followed by the smaller ones. Fit the cover plate and three screws (with countersunk or cheese-heads). Now test the roller race for freeness on its track and apply a little medium grease or anti-centrifuge grease.

Check all the clutch plates on the body and in the sprocket (clutch case) for freeness. Next fit the sprocket to the body, revolve the sprocket on the race to check free movement, and fit all the plates in the following sequence.

First a double-sided bonded driven plate, followed by a plain driving plate and so on in alternate order until the last bonded plate (single-sided) is fitted. This should present its plain steel side to the pressure plate. Fit the clutch to the gearbox mainshaft, fit the spring washer and nut, engage top gear, and tighten the nut.

Finally fit the clutch push-rod, the clutch pressure plate, the spring cups, the springs, and the spring adjuster nuts. Screw up the nuts until the studs are flush with the ends of the nuts, and adjust as necessary to ensure square withdrawal of the clutch pressure plate. Replace the outer portion of the oil-bath chain case as described on page 99.

To Remove Burman Gearbox Outer Cover (1955-6). First remove the kick-starter crank by loosening the pinch-bolt and pulling the crank off. Next detach the foot gear-change indicator by unscrewing the centre bolt from the spindle. Also remove the gear-change lever by unscrewing its pinch-bolt and pulling the lever off the shaft splines. Now remove all the cheese-headed screws which secure the gearbox outer cover and very carefully withdraw the cover. Be careful not to tear the paper washer used for the joint. If this is damaged during removal, renew it at once. Should the joint be difficult to break, do not attempt to prise the cover off, but apply a punch at the extremities where the outer cover overhangs the inner cover (on all recent gearboxes).

Note that the removal of the outer cover necessarily involves the loss of some oil which must be replenished through the clutch-worm inspection hole until oil begins to drip from the level-plug hole which is normally plugged by the square-headed level plug situated to the rear of and on the same level as the kick-starter crank. When the outer cover is replaced, tighten all the cheese-headed securing screws lightly and then firmly in opposite pairs.

To Remove Burman Gearbox from Frame (1955–6). Remove the gearbox outer-cover carefully. Also release the clutch control-cable from its operating arm by rotating the worm with a large screwdriver. Detach the cable adjuster from the inner cover. Now remove the oil-bath outer portion, the clutch, and engine sprocket (*see* page 99). Removal of the nut securing the engine sprocket is facilitated by engaging bottom gear and getting someone to hold the rear wheel while the nut is being spannered.

Remove the inner portion of the oil-bath (*see* page 97), the secondary-chain guard, and the secondary chain. Also remove the nut and adjuster bolt from the off-side of the gearbox top-bolt and extract the bolt from the near-side. Detach the spring from the prop stand, and also the nut from the off-side of the gearbox bottom-bolt. Remove the nut and tap out the bolt. Now swing the gearbox round in an anti-clockwise direction and lift it out of the frame on the off-side.

To Remove A.M.C. Gearbox from Frame (1957–8). First remove the oil-bath chain case and the clutch. Also remove the kick-starter crank, the gear indicator, the gear lever, the clutch lever inspection, and the oil filler cover.

Disconnect the clutch inner wire from the clutch operating lever, unscrew the cable adjuster and remove. Remove the gearbox top and bottom bolts. Swing the A.M.C. gearbox round until its fixing points lie approximately horizontal, and manoeuvre the gearbox out through the off-side of the frame.

To Remove AMC Gearbox from Frame (1959–62). With the featherbed type frame it is not possible to remove the gearbox as a separate unit. The whole design is based on an engine/gearbox unit as an integral part. If for any reason it is necessary for the gearbox shell to be removed, lift the engine/gearbox assembly from the frame as described on page 88. The gearbox can then be removed as a subsequent operation.

GENERAL MAINTENANCE

Gearbox Overhaul. Provided that the gearbox is kept properly topped-up with engine oil (*see* page 35) and reasonable care is taken when gear changing, a gearbox overhaul should not be necessary until a very big mileage has been covered. If the gearbox eventually becomes noisy and gear changing difficult, it is advisable to remove the gearbox from the frame (1955-8) models, or from the engine (1959-62 models) and have it thoroughly overhauled by the makers or a reputable repairer. As gearbox overhaul is rather beyond the average Norton owner, appropriate dismantling, inspection, and assembling instructions are not included in this section. For detailed instructions, you are referred to those given in the official Norton instruction book issued with each new machine.

WHEELS, BRAKES, AND TYRES

No Adjustment for Wheel Bearings. No adjustment is necessary or provided for the journal-type bearings fitted to the wheel hubs of 1955-62 Norton models.

Removing Front Wheel (1955-9 Models). Place the Norton on both stands or on the centre stand and disconnect the front-brake cable from the cam lever. Also disconnect the cable adjuster from the brake plate. Remove the off-side wheel-spindle nut, and loosen the pinch-bolt in the near-side fork end. With the left hand, support the front wheel and withdraw the spindle, using a tommy-bar inserted through the hole in the spindle head.

Fitting Front Wheel (1955-9 Models). Follow the reverse order of dismantling. The spindle should be inserted from the near-side. After tightening the spindle nut, lock the pinch-bolt in the near-side fork end.

Front Wheel Removal (1960-2). Place the motor-cycle on its central stand; remove the split pin from the brake control clevis pin and withdraw the pin. Unscrew the cable adjuster from the brake plate. Also unscrew the wheel spindle nut (R.H. thread) and release the pinch stud nut in the left-hand fork end.

Take the weight of the wheel in the left hand and withdraw the spindle by means of a tommy-bar placed through the hole in the head of the spindle. Remove the spindle and as the wheel is withdrawn, take great care not to allow the brake plate to fall from the drum. If allowed to fall, the bevelled edge can be seriously damaged. Place the spindle and dust cover in a clean receptacle to prevent contamination with grit.

Replacing Front Wheel (1960-2). Reassemble in the reverse order of dismantling. Fit the brake plate into the drum, and as the wheel is lifted into the telescopic forks, position the dust cover on the left-hand side and make sure that the torque stop on the brake plate engages the slot in the right-hand fork leg. With the right hand pass the spindle through and replace and tighten the spindle nut. Deflect the telescopic forks several times to "centre" the near-side leg on the spindle. Do not over-tighten the pinch stud nut on the left-hand side. The lug on the fork leg can be broken if this stud is over tightened. Finally reconnect and adjust the front brake cable.

Removing Rear Wheel (Spring Frame, 1955 Models). On the 1955 Models 19 and ES2 Nortons with "swinging arm" rear suspension, the rear wheel is of the quickly-detachable type. Disconnect the stop tail lamp leads by pulling the cable either side of the rubber-covered snap connector behind the rear number plate. Then remove the rear mudguard tail-piece by taking out the two bolts which secure it to the main portion of the mudguard, also the two bolts at the bottom of the tail-piece holding the stays.

Detach the speedometer driving cable. Remove the wheel spindle, distance piece, and speedometer driving box. Next remove the nuts from the hub studs and draw the wheel clear of the three studs, and the wheel will come right away, leaving the brake drum in position.

The procedure for removing the rear wheel, complete with brake drum, is to remove the mudguard tail-piece, disconnect the secondary chain, remove the anchorage bolt securing the brake anchorage arm to the frame, remove the brake-rod adjuster nut, loosen the wheel-spindle nuts, and then ease the wheel out of the frame fork-ends.

Replacing Rear Wheel (Spring Frame, 1955). To replace the quickly-detachable rear wheel on Model ES2 or 191 with "swinging arm" rear suspension, reverse the procedure used for removing the wheel. When the wheel is replaced in the fork-ends, see that the hub spindle is hard up against the chain adjusters. When replacing the chain spring-link always verify that its *closed* end faces the direction of chain motion, and check that the tension of the chain (*see* page 94) is correct if the chain drawbolt-adjuster nuts (*B*, Fig. 54) have been disturbed. In this case, also verify that both wheels are in true alignment, and check the adjustment of the rear-brake pedal.

Tighten both wheel-spindle nuts firmly and also connect up securely the speedometer driving-cable. Finally tighten down the hinged tail-piece of the rear mudguard and see that the stop-tail lamp leads are properly reconnected with the snap connector.

Removing Rear Wheel (1955–9 Models). On the 1956 Models ES2, 19, and 50 with full-width light-alloy rear hubs and "swinging arm" rear suspension, a quickly-detachable rear wheel is provided. This can be readily removed as described below.

First place the machine on its centre stand and disconnect the tail and stop-light leads by pulling each cable either side of the rubber-covered snap-on connector located behind the rear number plate. Next remove the end bolt from each side lifting-handle. This enables the mudguard hinged tail-piece to be readily lifted when the rear wheel is withdrawn. Disconnect the speedometer driving cable.

Now remove the three rubber plugs from the end of the wheel hub, thereby exposing the sleeve-nuts which retain the wheel. With a suitable box spanner remove the sleeve nuts. Also remove the rear wheel spindle and distance-piece. Then withdraw the rear wheel from the retaining studs, leaving the rear-brake drum and the secondary chain undisturbed.

If it is desired to remove the rear wheel together with the brake drum, disconnect the secondary chain and remove the chain guard. Also remove the knurled adjuster-nut on the end of the brake rod, disconnect the brake torque arm (1955–8) from the frame, and disconnect the speedometer drive. Then release the wheel spindle and nut from the near-side stub axle so as to enable the rear wheel to be slid along the adjusting slots and withdrawn.

Replacing Rear Wheel (1955–9 Models). Replace the wheel in the reverse order of dismantling. Do not forget to fit the spring link on the chain with the open end facing *away from* the direction of chain movement. Also check that the chain adjuster-plates are correctly seated, and that the chain is tensioned so that there is about $\frac{3}{4}$ in. slackness (total up-and-down movement) in the centre of the chain lower run, with the chain in its tightest position and with the rear shock-absorbers compressed to mid-stroke. Check the rear brake adjustment, and if necessary, wheel alignment.

Removing Rear Wheel (1960 Onwards). Place the motor-cycle on its centre stand. On de Luxe models only, remove the rear number plate. Remove the three rubber plugs from the off-side of the rear hub and with a box or socket spanner remove the three sleeve nuts thus exposed. Unscrew the right-hand portion of the wheel spindle and withdraw. Remove the spacer and speedometer drive gearbox, and allow the latter to hang on its cable. Withdraw the rear wheel from the brake drum by pulling it to the off-side; it should come clear of the brake drum which will be left in position.

All recent standard type Nortons do *not* have a detachable rear mudguard portion and it is therefore necessary to stand on the nearside and incline the machine slightly toward you on the stand. The rear wheel can then be withdrawn with the right hand from the off-side.

On de Luxe models if the tyre is punctured and therefore flat, the wheel can be withdrawn rearwards through the space left by the removal of the number plate. With the tyre inflated, it may be necessary to incline the machine as for standard type models to get the wheel clear. Should it be necessary to remove the rear wheel complete with brake, remove the secondary chain case or guard and disconnect the chain. Remove the brake rod adjusting nut but do not push the brake pedal down to withdraw the rod from the roller.

Disconnect the "dead" lead from the stop-lamp switch. Also disconnect the speedometer drive cable and slacken both sides of the wheel spindle. The wheel should now slide out of the rear fork ends. Remove it as previously described, but note that it may be necessary to remove the off-side silencer due to greater width caused by the off-side portion of the wheel spindle remaining in the hub.

Replacing Rear Wheel (1960 Onwards). Reverse the dismantling procedure and, if fitting with brake complete, make sure that the torque stop on the brake plate engages properly with the slot in the left-hand fork end. Engage the brake rod in the cam lever roller and push the wheel spindle up against the adjuster screws. Position the speedometer gearbox for correct cable take-off angle and tighten both sides of the spindle. Connect the speedometer drive cable, but do not over tighten the gland nut. Replace the secondary chain, being careful to fit the spring link correctly. Check the tension of the secondary chain (*see* page 95). Replace the chain case or the chain guard and adjust the rear brake. Reconnect the stop switch "dead" lead. On de Luxe models refit the number plate.

When replacing the rear wheel only, with the brake drum already *in situ*, incline the machine as necessary to position the rear wheel under the mudguard or tail fairing. Turn the brake drum by hand so that one of the three studs is approximately in line with the pivoted fork (swinging arm). This assists getting the bearing boss on the hub past the other two studs and fitting the hub to the rear brake drum.

Fit and tighten the three sleeve nuts and replace the rubber plugs. Fit the speedometer drive gearbox, being sure that its driving dogs properly engage with the slots in the hub bearing lock ring. Position the spacer and fit the right-hand part of the divided spindle. Be careful to see that the washer on this passes the end of the adjuster screw in the fork end, and that as the spindle is screwed home its head does not catch on the adjuster screw and bend it. Tighten the spindle and on de Luxe models refit the number plate.

The Hub Bearings. As has been stated on page 105, *no adjustment* is provided or necessary.

Dismantling the Hubs. Dismantling is rarely necessary, but should it become necessary to dismantle a hub, follow the instructions given in the maker's Manual.

Adjusting the Brakes. If the brakes are used too frequently and heavily, the friction linings are apt to wear, and adjustment becomes necessary.

GENERAL MAINTENANCE

In the case of the rear internal-expanding brake there are two separate adjustments on most models.

In addition to provision for taking up lining wear, an independent adjustment is provided for altering the angle of the brake-pedal lever; thus in all positions of the adjustable footrests the brake can be conveniently operated without removing the foot from the rest. The adjuster nut located at the end of the brake rod should be turned *clockwise* to remedy wear. To alter the angle of the brake-pedal lever, proceed thus: loosen the rod adjuster-nut, slacken the brake-pedal stop lock-nut (*B*, Fig. 60),

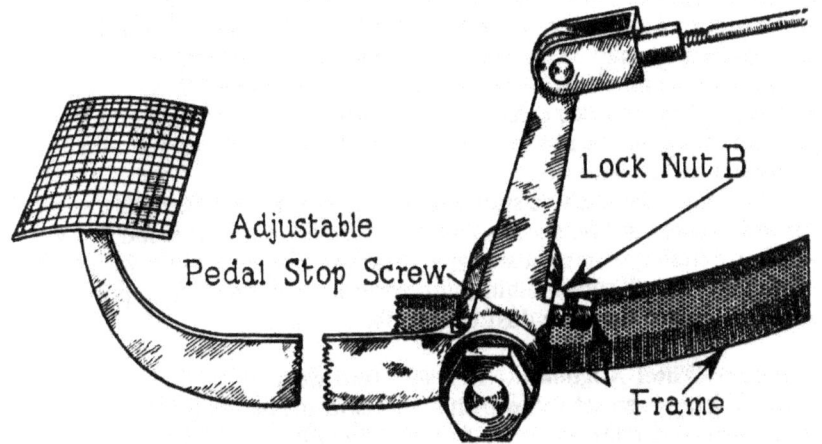

FIG. 60. THE DUAL ADJUSTMENT FOR THE REAR BRAKE

Comprising an adjustable pedal stop and a nut (not shown) at the rear end of the brake-rod.

and adjust the hexagon-headed stop-screw to obtain the best pedal position. Afterwards retighten the lock-nut and adjust the brake rod adjuster-nut as required. Place the gear pedal in neutral and tighten the adjuster-nut until the minimum amount of pedal movement operates the brake without, however, any suspicion of friction when the pedal is released and the wheel is rotated by hand.

As regards front brake adjustment finger adjustment is provided on many models; the adjuster located at the lower end of the operating cable may be screwed *outwards* as necessary to maintain minimum clearance between the brake linings and the brake drum, until such time as the operation of the handlebar lever results in the cam lever moving beyond its best position, i.e. a right-angle between the brake cable and lever.

Now disconnect the cable "U" clip and remove the cam lever. Turn the lever over and refit. This will restore the lever to something like the position it originally occupied and will provide a new lease of life.

Brake Linings. If either brake is harsh in action or tends to squeak, remove the anchor plate and file each lining thin for about 1 in. from each end. This slightly reduces the effective area of the brake lining but results in much smoother braking without any appreciable decrease in efficiency. Smooth hard linings should be roughened up with a file, and oily ones cleaned with petrol.

Tyres. Check the tyre inflation pressures (*see* page 4) about once a week and, if found low, pump up to the requisite lb per sq in., using a pressure gauge. Never ride your motor-cycle with the rear tyre deflated, as the fabric of the cover, as well as the tube, suffers severely if this is done, and the damage may be almost irreparable. From time to time inspect the covers with the machine jacked up, and remove all small flints with a sharp penknife. This practice often saves a hold-up on the road, as flints which get embedded in the rubber usually penetrate deeper as the machine is continued to be run.

Never leave the machine standing for a long time unjacked, as this is bad for both wheels and tyres. Also avoid letting the machine stand in a welter of oil or paraffin, which causes tyres to soften and deteriorate very rapidly. Note that "Butyl" tubes retain full pressure much longer than pure rubber tubes. Replace the valve dust cap if lost.

Sidecar Wheel Alignment. If heavy tyre wear and skidding are to be avoided, it is essential to keep the wheels in proper alignment relative to each other and relative to the frame. The adjuster screws or draw-bolt-adjuster nuts (pre-1956 spring frame) at the chain stays should be adjusted evenly on both sides.

When fitting or refitting a Norton sidecar, place the sidecar in position, leaving all attachment bolts slack. The sidecar wheel should not run parallel with the machine wheels, or there would be a tendency for the machine to constantly pull to the left. The sidecar wheel should toe-in towards the machine ¾ in. (*see* Fig. 61).

Alignment is regulated by the clip-lug at the bottom of the sidecar centre arm, and the clip lug of the rear arm. To align correctly, two boards about 6 ft long, 4 in. wide, and 1 in. thick are necessary, which should be placed on the floor, one against the two tyres of the machine, the other against the one tyre of the sidecar. Now measure the distance between the boards immediately in front of the front wheel and at the rear of the rear wheel; the distance between the edges should be ¾ in. less at the front than at the rear.

Besides checking the wheels for track, it is desirable to check that the motor-cycle is correctly aligned in a vertical plane. Fig. 62 suggests the best method of verifying this point. Place the outfit on a level floor and then lay a board (about 4 ft long) against the upper part of the front forks on each side of the machine, as indicated. Mark where the board touches

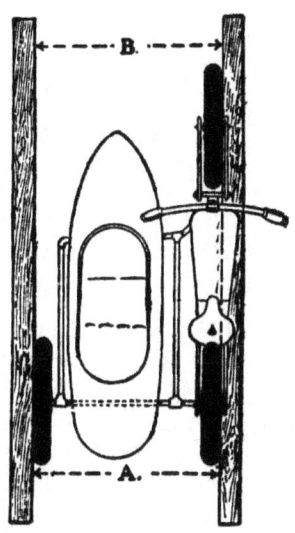

FIG. 61. SIDECAR ALIGNMENT

The distance B should be $\frac{3}{4}$ in. less than the distance A.

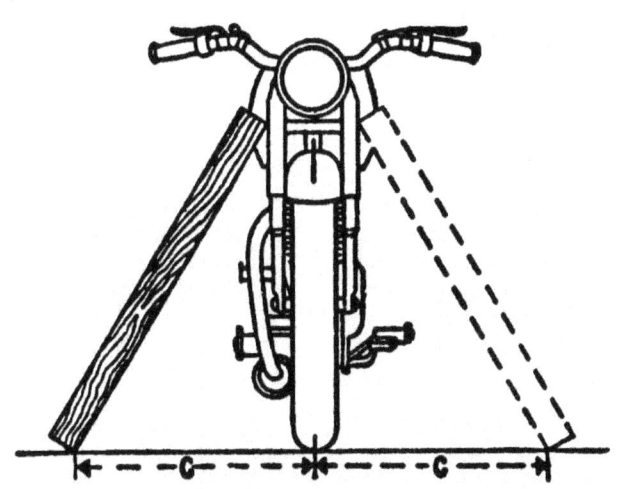

FIG. 62. HOW TO CHECK IF THE MOTOR-CYCLE OF A SIDECAR OUTFIT IS VERTICAL

the floor and then measure the two dimensions C. It is assumed the board has a straight edge and is rested in the same position on each side of the forks. If the motor-cycle itself is truly vertical, the two dimensions C will, of course, be exactly equal. It is recommended, however, that the motor-cycle itself leans slightly *away* from the sidecar. In this case dimension C on the off-side should be slightly greater than dimension C on the near-side. An excessive outward lean is to be deprecated and is bad for the outfit and its driver. Norton Motors Ltd., recommend a ¾ in. lean over the height of the motor-cycle, measured on a plumb line.

Fitting a Sidecar to a "Featherbed" Frame (1959 Onwards). It is necessary to *reduce the trail* to ensure good handling. A special fork crown and column, and head clip, are available. Because these have different dimensions, new top fork covers with lamp brackets are required. These parts reduce the trail and with an outfit properly aligned and set up, produce excellent steering. The special fork crown and column requires a steering damper with two friction discs which centre on a large diameter boss on the underside of the crown. These parts do not affect the solo crown. There is also a steering damper for the solo crown which has a single friction disc of different dimensions, and when ordering parts it is important to state for which crown a damper is required.

Stronger front fork springs and rear shock-absorber springs are also available, and should be fitted. Because of the added electrical consumption of a sidecar lamp or lamps, an A.C. generator may not maintain the battery state unless an increased output is obtained as described on page 25.

Solo Wheel Alignment. To check the wheel alignment on a solo motor-cycle, use a straight-edged board (about 6 ft long, 1 in. wide, and ½ in. thick), or a taut piece of string. Place the motor-cycle on its stand so that it is quite upright. Then check for correct alignment by holding the straight edge or board in contact with the front and rear tyres. If the wheel alignment is correct, the straight edge or board should contact *each tyre* at the *front and rear*. Rectify faulty alignment by means of the chain adjusters in the rear fork ends (*see* page 95). Take into account the fact that 1959–62 front and rear tyres are 3·00 × 19 and 3·50 × 19 respectively.

STEERING HEAD, ADJUSTMENT

Steering-head Adjustment (1955–59 Forks). Raise the front wheel clear of the ground by placing a suitable box under the engine cradle. Then place the thumb of the left hand on the joint between the steering head and the fork-head clip. Endeavour to lift the front forks with the right hand, when any play in the steering-head races should easily be detected.

If an adjustment is needed, slacken the steering column lock-nut, and also the pinch-bolt which clamps each fork leg to the fork crown. Remove

GENERAL MAINTENANCE

steering-head slackness by adjusting the nut on the steering column below the head clip. Make sure that the telescopic forks are quite free to rotate on the head races and, when the required adjustment has been made, re-tighten the steering column lock-nut and the two pinch-bolts.

Steering Head Adjustment (1960-2). With your Model ES2 or 50 jacked up on its centre stand, check that the front wheel is clear of the ground. If it is not, pack up the stand with a piece of wood. You can position the fingers of the left hand at the rear of the steel shroud which surrounds the headlug against the dust cover on the top of the bearing and against the back of the lug. To do this it may be necessary to remove the petrol tank (*see* page 63). Now with the right hand, take hold of the front mudguard and pull and push fore and aft. Should the bearings be slack, you can feel movement between the dust cover and headlug.

The head ballraces are of the crowded ball type designed to carry an end load. Therefore they should be slightly pre-loaded, but not sufficiently to prevent the handlebars "falling" from the central position to either lock when the front wheel is clear of the ground.

To adjust the steering head, slacken the plated dome nut on top of the steering column. In order to use a good fitting spanner of the ring or box type it is desirable to remove the handlebars from their mounting clips. Slacken the dome nut only slightly, just sufficient to permit the adjuster nut below the head clip to be moved. An open-ended spanner must, of course, be used for this purpose. A suitable spanner is available from the Norton Service Dept. (Part No. SPUI/49). This also fits the fork filler plugs which have the same hexagon.

Loosen the nuts on the pinch studs which clamp the fork main tubes in the crown. Adjust as necessary, tighten the column nut, and check again. When you have obtained the correct steering head adjustment, do not forget to tighten the pinch stud nuts.

A Thief-proof Locking Arrangement. On solo models (1960-62) an abutment on the bottom left-hand side of the steering head, and a hole on the left-hand side of the fork crown, permit a padlock to be fitted which will lock the steering on *full right lock*.

TELESCOPIC FORKS AND REAR SPRINGING

Maintenance of Telescopic Front Forks. Little maintenance is necessary other than to occasionally replenish the damping oil as described on page 38. This maintenance is very important, and it is essential to use the correct type of damping oil. The front fork inwards are made pretty tough as they have to withstand tough usage. Only after a very big mileage or after riding frequently over rough terrain is it necessary to remove the front forks from the frame and dismantle the forks for inspection and renewal of parts. The removal of the front forks is dealt with in this

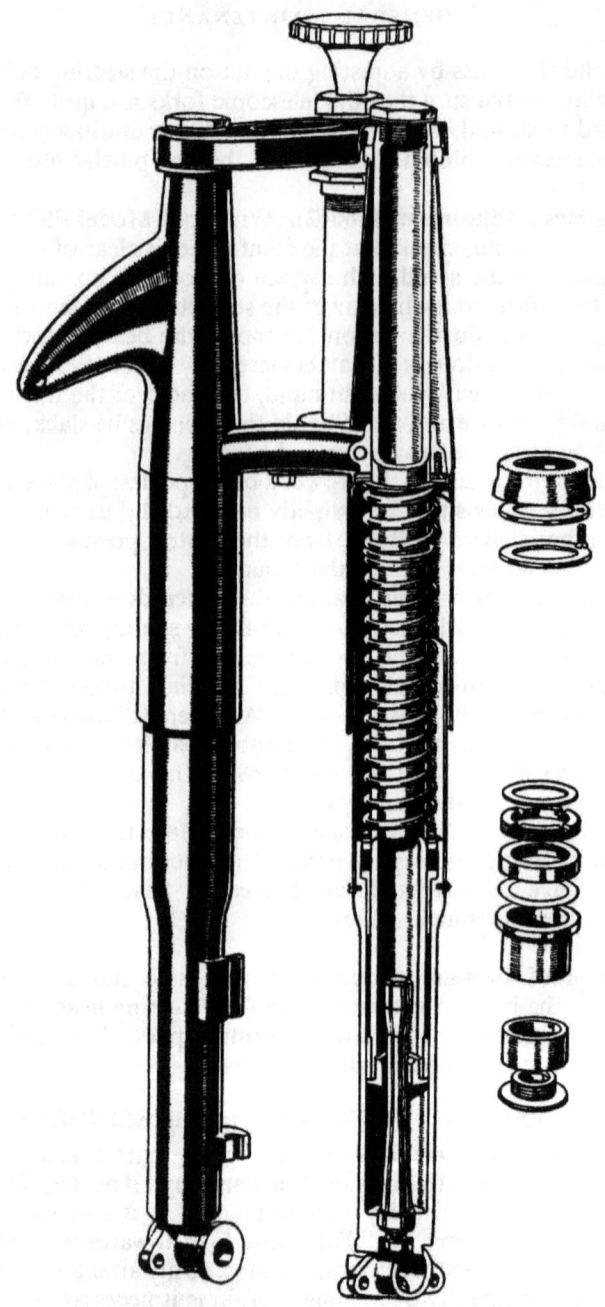

Fig. 63. Telescopic Front Forks (1955–58)

GENERAL MAINTENANCE 115

section, but their dismantling and reassembly are not covered. Should dismantling and inspection be considered necessary, refer to the official maker's Maintenance Manual.

Removing 1955–58 Forks from Frame. The front wheel and mudguard can, if desired, be left in position. First detach the wiring from the headlamp and remove the steering-damper arm from the frame. Also disconnect the speedometer lighting and driving cables from the speedometer head. Disconnect all control cables from the handlebars and remove the latter.

Completely slacken the steering damper, and remove the steering column lock-nut, complete with damper rod and knob. Next take off the oil fillerplugs and the speedometer panel. Remove the steering-head clip and head race adjusting nut. Then withdraw the telescopic forks, being careful not to lose any balls from the steering-head races. Also avoid spilling any damping oil from the fork legs. If this happens, subsequent replenishment (see page 38) will be necessary.

Fitting 1955–59 Forks to Frame. First inspect the steering-head races and balls. There should be 17 balls per race. If the races are pitted, knock them out of their housings and renew. With regard to the races in the frame, each has a small hole provided to permit the entry of grease. See that this is clear. Grease generously the track of the race fitted to the base of the steering column, and the top frame-race. Position the 34 balls and gently insert the steering column through the frame head.

Position the top race and dust cover, and then screw the adjusting nut down the column until the hexagon is bearing lightly against the top race. Now replace the steering-head clip and the speedometer panel. Also fit loosely the steering column locking-nut, and fit and tighten firmly both filler plugs. Afterwards adjust the steering head correctly (see page 112), replace the remaining items, and check all nuts and bolts for security.

Removing Front Forks (1959 Onwards). Place your Model ES2 or 50 on its centre stand, or place a stout wooden box beneath the engine. Free the clutch and brake cables from the handlebar levers. Remove the handlebar clips and allow the handlebars to rest on the petrol tank. Unscrew both the filler plugs located on the top of the telescopic fork legs. Pull the front forks and wheel upwards and place a block of wood or a suitable tin beneath the front tyre so as to keep the wheel up when unscrewing the filler plugs from the top of the damper rods. A thin $\frac{5}{16}$ Whit. open-ended spanner is required for this, together with the filler plug spanner.

Remove the filler plugs with their washers. Also remove the Lucas prefocus headlamp and allow it to hang by the cables. Now disconnect the front brake cable from the brake plate and remove the front wheel. Remove the top column nut and give the headclip a sharp jar upwards with a mallet to free it from tapers on the main tubes. Next remove the headlamp clip, followed by the top covers with the lamp brackets and their rubber washers.

Note that it is necessary on some 1960 and 1961 machines to remove the

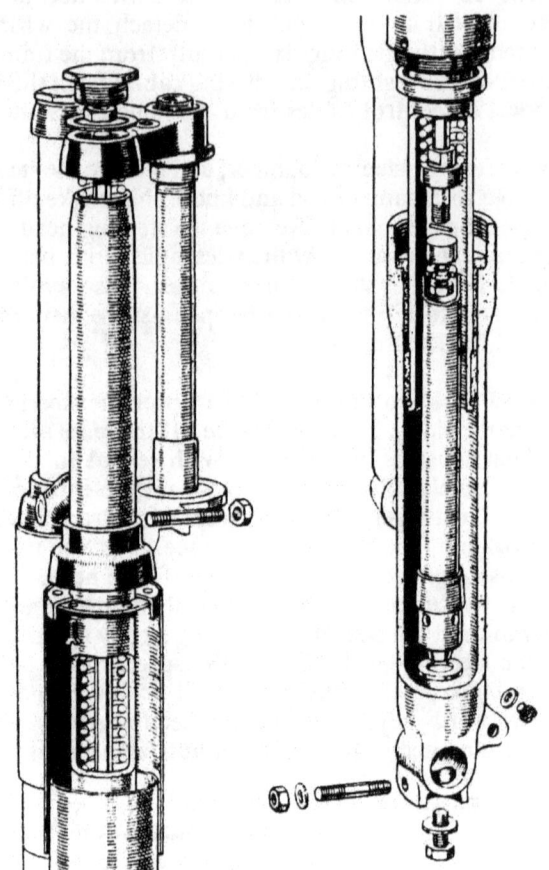

FIG. 64. TELESCOPIC FRONT FORKS (1959 ONWARDS)
On the left is shown the upper half and on the right the lower half.

steering lock stop plate before the steering column can be withdrawn, and this applies to 1962 models if they are fitted with steering dampers. This is secured with a single $\frac{5}{16}$ in. × 26T bolt with washers, spacer, and nut, to the trouser plate on the frame immediately below the headlug. Remove the steering column nut and dust cover, and carefully withdraw the telescopic front forks.

Replacing Front Forks (1959 Onwards). Pack the head ball races with grease and press a felt washer into the side of each race. These washers must be fitted in the side with the wider gap between the inner and outer races. The races must then be fitted in the frame with the felt washers *outwards*. When the headlug is viewed from above and below the washers should be clearly visible. See that the shim washer is positioned on the base of the steering column. Insert the steering column through the headlug bearings. Fit the top shim washer, the dust cover, and screw down the column nut. Replace the headlamp brackets, their top rubber washers, and headclip. Release the nuts in the pinch studs in the fork crown. Adjust the steering head bearings and tighten the top column nut. See that this does not alter the bearing setting.

Pull up the telescopic front forks to expose the springs and damper rods. Fit the filler plugs and washers to the damper rods. First make certain that the lock-nuts are already screwed down to the end of the thread on the rod. Tighten the filler plugs to pull the main tubes into their tapers in the headclip, and tighten the pinch-studs on the crown.

It is assumed that the damping oil in the front fork legs has not been drained off if the front forks were removed complete with the front mudguard and stays in position. Replace the Lucas headlamp, the handlebars, and front wheel. Then reconnect the control cables. Finally check the headlamp for correct height and see that its beam is properly aligned (*see* page 19).

Rear Springing (1955-8 Models). In the case of the "swinging arm" and shock absorber units fitted to 1955-8 spring-frame models, *no maintenance* whatever is normally needed (*see* page 39) and in the unlikely event of any attention being necessary, the shock absorber units should be removed and taken to the nearest Norton dealer or distributor. Removal of the units is straightforward. The "swinging arm" pivot requires neither lubrication nor adjustment, but after a big mileage the Silentbloc bushes (*see* page 118) may require to be renewed.

Removing and Dismantling "Swinging Arm" (1955-58). Should dismantling become necessary after a big mileage in order to renew the Silentbloc bushes, do this in the following manner. First remove the rear wheel, as described on page 106. Next take off the shock absorber units after removing the bolts which secure the top and bottom members to the frame and "swinging arm" respectively (*see* Fig. 65). Remove the outer portion of the oil-bath chain case (*see* page 96) and also the clutch (*see* page 99); remove the nut from the off-side of the pivot bolt. Then drift out the pivot bolt and withdraw the "swinging arm."

To Remove Silentbloc Bushes (1955-58). To remove the bushes from the "swinging arm," knock them out with a suitable drift. This should have a diameter only slightly smaller than the inside diameter of the cross tube. Its length must be greater than the hole in the Silentbloc outer-sleeve. If difficulty is experienced in removing the bushes, soak them in suitable oil.

To Assemble and Replace "Swinging Arm" (1955–58). Drift or press one new Silentbloc bush into the "swinging arm" until its outer sleeve is

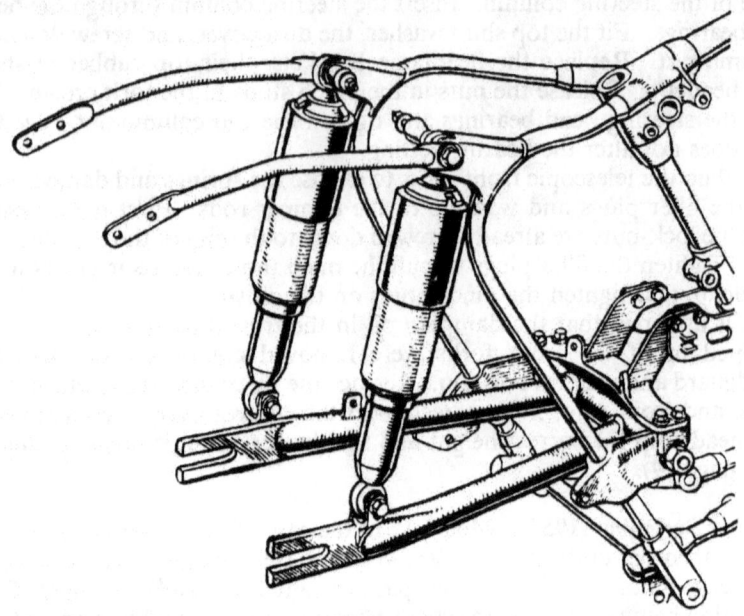

FIG. 65. THE "SWINGING ARM" AND SHOCK ABSORBERS (1955–8)

(*By courtesy of " Motor Cycle," London*)

level with the extremity of the cross tube. From the opposite side insert the distance-piece and drift or press right home the second Silentbloc bush. Then position the "swinging arm," being careful to see that the brackets for attaching are on the top side (*see* Fig. 65). Finally replace the pivot bolt, fit the nut, and securely tighten it.

"Swinging Arm" Removal and Assembly (1959). This is rarely necessary. However, at very long intervals it may be desirable to renew the Silentbloc bushes. To remove the "swinging arm," proceed as follows. Remove the rear wheel (*see* page 106) and the shock-absorber units which are secured only by a single bolt and nut at each end. Remove the nut and washer from one end of the "swinging arm" bolt, withdraw the bolt, and remove the "swinging arm."

To renew the Silentbloc bushes, drift out one end, remove the tubular distance piece and drift out the remaining bush. Press in the new bush until the outer steel sleeve is flush with the end of the tube. Remember to replace the distance piece before inserting the second bush. When securing the "swinging arm" in position in the frame, a dimension of $11\frac{3}{8}$ in. should be taken from the hole forming the top absorber anchorage to the shock-absorber anchorage hole in the "swinging arm," the arm being held in this position while tightening the "swinging arm" pivot bolt.

"Swinging Arm" Removal and Assembly (1960 Onwards). Remove the chain case or chain guard. Next remove the rear wheel, complete with the rear brake. Remove the bottom shock-absorber attachment bolts, nuts, and washers. Swing the shock-absorbers clear and slacken the top bolts if necessary. Remove the nut and washer from one end of the pivotted fork bolt on the frame gusset plate and withdraw the bolt from the opposite side. The "swinging arm" should now be pushed forward to clear the gusset plates, turned and withdrawn.

Should it be found necessary to replace the "Clayflex" bearings return the "swinging arm" to the Service Dept. of Norton Motors Ltd or a Norton repair specialist.

To replace the "swinging arm," reverse the dismantling procedure. Fit and tighten the bottom shock-absorber bolts before tightening the "swinging arm" pivot bolt on the frame. This will ensure that the "Clayflex" bearings are clamped in approximately the correct rotational position.

The Shock-absorber Units (1959–62). These are sealed and leak-proof. *Do not interfere with them.* Removal is simple and in the most unlikely event of any attention becoming necessary, take the units to your usual Norton dealer or distributor. To promote silent operation it is permissible to remove the covers in order to grease the spring. Note that with the "C" spanner provided in the tool kit you can set the units in *three positions*. The soft or normal solo position is in use when the abutments spot welded to the damper body are in engagement with the topmost positions on the bottom spring collar which has a scroll or face cam, or when this part is rotated as far as possible in an *anti-clockwise* direction when viewed from above. Rotation in a *clockwise* direction by means of the key will result in the stronger positions being engaged. Make sure that both shock-absorber units are adjusted to the same position. Make no attempt whatever to dismantle, drain, or refill the units.

INDEX

ALTERNATOR, Lucas, 25
Amal carburettor, 40–9
Ammeter, 13

BATTERY—
  care of, 13–17
  connexions, 16
Brake—
  adjustment, 108–9
  lubrication, 39
Brushes, dynamo, 11
Bulb renewal, 20
Burman clutch parts, 101

CARBON, removing, 67
Carburettor, 40–9
Carburettor, dismantling, 48
Chain drive, contact-breaker, 29
Chains, 96
Cleaning—
  carburettor, 48
  chromium, 51
  enamel, 51
  engine and gearbox, 51
  lamps, 20
  "Magdyno" contacts, 56
  sparking plugs, 53–5
Clutch—
  adjustment, 91
  dismantling, 99–102
Coil, 27
Commutator, 11
Compensated voltage control, 12
Connecting-rod bearings, 88
Contact-breaker, 28–31
Controls, use of, 1, 5
Crankcase, draining, 35

DECARBONIZING, 61–75
Dipper switch, 24
Dynamo maintenance, 10–13

EMERGENCY starting, 25
Enamel, cleaning, 51

Engine and frame numbers, 50
Engine—
  oils, suitable, 33
  overhaul, 80
  removal, 88
Exhaust flame, 44
Exhaust valve lifter adjustment, 61

FLOAT chamber, 48
Front forks, 37, 113–17
Front wheel removal, 105
Fuel—
  consumption, high, 47
  replenishment, 3

GEAR changing, 7–8
Gearbox—
  lubrication, 35
  overhaul, 105
  removal, 104
Greases, suitable, 36
Grinding-in valves, 72

HEADLAMP position, adjusting, 19
Horn, 31
Hub lubrication, 38

IGNITION—
  lever cables, 57
  timing, 75–8

JET-NEEDLE, 47

LAMPS, 17–20
Lubrication—
  brake, 39
  control levers, 39
  engine, 32–5
  gearbox, 35
  "Magdyno," 35
  motor-cycle parts, 35–9
  primary chain, 36
  secondary chain, 36
  steering head, 36
  wheel hubs, 38

"MAGDYNO," removing, 80
Main jet, 41, 45

NEEDLE-JET, 41
Neutral, obtaining, 8

OIL—
  circulation, 6
  pump, 82
  replenishment, 3
  tank, draining, 34
Oil-bath chain case removal, 96–9
Oil-pressure control valve, 34, 83

PETROL tank removal, 62
Pilot—
  air screw, 41
  jet, 46
Piston—
  removal, 68
  rings, 69
  seizure, 9
Primary chain adjustment, 93
Push-rod adjustment, 60

REAR springing, 39, 117
Rear wheel removal, 106–8
Rectifier, 27
Retiming Lucas "Magdyno," 76
Riding position, 1
Rocker-box, dismantling, 85
Running-in, 9

SECONDARY chain—
  adjustment, 94–6
  lubrication, 36
Shock-absorber units, 119

Sidecar—
  fitting, 112
  wheel alignment, 110
Slip-ring, 58
Slow running, bad, 47
Small-end bush, 89
Solo wheel alignment, 112
Sparking plug—
  gap, 53
  types, 9
Specific gravity, checking, 14–17
Spring link, chain, 96
Starting up, 5
Steering head—
  adjustment, 112–13
  lubrication, 36
Stop-tail lamp, 19, 24, 28
"Swinging arm," 117–19
Switch positions, 18, 22

THROTTLE—
  stop, 40
  valve cut-away, 41, 46
Timing—
  cover, removing, 74
  gear bushes, 91
  gears, removing, 83
Topping-up battery, 14
Tyre pressures, 4
Tyres, 110

VALVE—
  clearances, 59–61
  guides, 72
  timing, 78
Valves, removing, 71

WHEEL alignment, 110–12
Wiring diagrams, 22, 23, 30

ARE YOU:
INTERESTED IN EUROPEAN, IMPORT & EXOTIC AUTOMOBILES?

DO YOU:
DO YOUR OWN MAINTENANCE?

If you answered yes to either of these questions, then you should check out our automobile books and manuals. We have included a sample listing of some of our featured marques. However, for complete details and the most up-to-date information, please visit our website.

——— www.VelocePress.com ———

The fastest growing specialist USA publisher of niche market automotive books and manuals.

All VelocePress titles are available through your local independent bookseller, Amazon.com or direct from VelocePress. Wholesale customers may also purchase direct or from the Ingram Book Group.

AUTOBOOKS WORKSHOP MANUALS

ALFA ROMEO GIULIA 1300, 1600, 1750, 2000 1962-1978 WSM
AUSTIN HEALEY SPRITE, MG MIDGET 1958-1980 WSM
BMW 1600 1966-1973 WSM
BMW 2000 & 2002 1966-1976 WSM
BMW 2500, 2800, 3.0 & 3.3 1968-1977 WSM
BMW 316, 320, 320i 1975-1977 WSM
BMW 518, 520, 520i 1973-1981 WSM
FIAT 1100, 1100D, 1100R & 1200 1957-1969 WSM
FIAT 124 1966-1974 WSM
FIAT 124 SPORT 1966-1975 WSM
FIAT 125 & 125 SPECIAL 1967-1973 WSM
FIAT 126, 126L, 126 DV, 126/650 & 126/650 DV 1972-1982 WSM
FIAT 127 SALOON, SPECIAL & SPORT, 900, 1050 1971-1981 WSM
FIAT 128 1969-1982 WSM
FIAT 1300, 1500 1961-1967 WSM
FIAT 131 MIRAFIORI 1975-1982 WSM
FIAT 132 1972-1982 WSM
FIAT 500 1957-1973 WSM
FIAT 600, 600D & MULTIPLA 1955-1969 WSM
FIAT 850 1964-1972 WSM
JAGUAR E-TYPE 1961-1972 WSM
JAGUAR MK 1, 2 1955-1969 WSM
JAGUAR S TYPE, 420 1963-1968 WSM
JAGUAR XK 120, 140, 150 MK 7, 8, 9 1948-1961 WSM
LAND ROVER 1, 2 1948-1961 WSM
MERCEDES-BENZ 190 1959-1968 WSM
MERCEDES-BENZ 220/8 1968-1972 WSM
MERCEDES-BENZ 220B 1959-1965 WSM
MERCEDES-BENZ 230 1963-1968 WSM
MERCEDES-BENZ 250 1968-1972 WSM
MERCEDES-BENZ 280 1968-1972 WSM
MG MIDGET TA-TF 1936-1955 WSM
MINI 1959-1980 WSM
MORRIS MINOR 1952-1971 WSM
PEUGEOT 404 1960-1975 WSM
PORSCHE 911 1964-1973 WSM
PORSCHE 911 1970-1977 WSM
RENAULT 16 1965-1979 WSM
RENAULT 8, 10, 1100 1962-1971 WSM
ROVER 3500, 3500S 1968-1976 WSM
SUNBEAM RAPIER, ALPINE 1955-1965 WSM
TRIUMPH SPITFIRE, GT6, VITESSE 1962-1968 WSM
TRIUMPH TR2, TR3, TR3A 1952-1962 WSM
TRIUMPH TR4, TR4A 1961-1967 WSM
VOLKSWAGEN BEETLE 1968-1977 WSM

BROOKLANDS BOOKS & ROAD TEST PORTFOLIOS (RTP)

AC CARS 1904-2009
ALFA ROMEO 1920-1933 ROAD TEST PORTFOLIO
ALFA ROMEO 1934-1940 ROAD TEST PORTFOLIO
BRABHAM RALT HONDA THE RON TAURANAC STORY
BUGATTI TYPE 10 TO TYPE 40 ROAD TEST PORTFOLIO
BUGATTI TYPE 10 TO TYPE 251 ROAD TEST PORTFOLIO
BUGATTI TYPE 41 TO TYPE 55 ROAD TEST PORTFOLIO
BUGATTI TYPE 57 TO TYPE 251 ROAD TEST PORTFOLIO
DELAHAYE ROAD TEST PORTFOLIO
FERRARI ROAD CARS 1946-1956 ROAD TEST PORTFOLIO
FIAT 500 1936-1972 ROAD TEST PORTFOLIO
FIAT DINO ROAD TEST PORTFOLIO
HISPANO SUIZA ROAD TEST PORTFOLIO
HONDA ST1100/ST1300 PAN EUROPEAN 1990-2002 RTP
JAGUAR MK1 & MK2 ROAD TEST PORTFOLIO
LOTUS CORTINA ROAD TEST PORTFOLIO
MV AGUSTA F4 750 & 1000 1997-2007 ROAD TEST PORTFOLIO
TATRA CARS ROAD TEST PORTFOLIO

VELOCEPRESS AUTOMOBILE BOOKS & MANUALS

ABARTH BUYERS GUIDE
AUSTIN-HEALEY 6-CYLINDER WSM
BMW 600 LIMOUSINE FACTORY WSM
BMW 600 LIMOUSINE OWNERS HAND BOOK & SERVICE MANUAL
BMW ISETTA FACTORY WSM
BOOK OF THE CARRERA PANAMERICANA - MEXICAN ROAD RACE
COMPLETE CATALOG OF JAPANESE MOTOR VEHICLES
DIALED IN - THE JAN OPPERMAN STORY
FERRARI 250/GT SERVICE AND MAINTENANCE
FERRARI 308 SERIES BUYER'S AND OWNER'S GUIDE
FERRARI BERLINETTA LUSSO
FERRARI BROCHURES AND SALES LITERATURE 1946-1967
FERRARI BROCHURES AND SALES LITERATURE 1968-1989
FERRARI GUIDE TO PERFORMANCE
FERRARI OPP, MAINTENANCE & SERVICE H/BOOKS 1948-1963
FERRARI OWNER'S HANDBOOK
FERRARI SERIAL NUMBERS PART I - ODD NUMBERS TO 21399
FERRARI SERIAL NUMBERS PART II - EVEN NUMBERS TO 1050
FERRARI SPYDER CALIFORNIA
FERRARI TUNING TIPS & MAINTENANCE TECHNIQUES
HENRY'S FABULOUS MODEL "A" FORD
HOW TO BUILD A FIBERGLASS CAR
HOW TO BUILD A RACING CAR
HOW TO RESTORE THE MODEL 'A' FORD
IF HEMINGWAY HAD WRITTEN A RACING NOVEL
JAGUAR E-TYPE 3.8 & 4.2 WSM
LE MANS 24 (THE BOOK THAT THE FILM WAS BASED ON)
MASERATI BROCHURES AND SALES LITERATURE
MASERATI OWNER'S HANDBOOK
METROPOLITAN FACTORY WSM
MGA & MGB OWNERS HANDBOOK & WSM
OBERT'S FIAT GUIDE
PERFORMANCE TUNING THE SUNBEAM TIGER
PORSCHE 356 1948-1965 WSM
PORSCHE 912 WSM
SOUPING THE VOLKSWAGEN
TRIUMPH TR2, TR3, TR4 1953-1965 WSM
VEDA ORR'S NEW REVISED HOT ROD PICTORIAL
VOLKSWAGEN TRANSPORTER, TRUCKS, STATION WAGONS WSM
VOLVO 1944-1968 ALL MODELS WSM

VELOCEPRESS MOTORCYCLE BOOKS & MANUALS

AJS SINGLES 1955-65 350cc & 500cc (BOOK OF)
ARIEL 1939-1960 4 STROKE SINGLES (BOOK OF)
ARIEL LEADER & ARROW 1958-1964 (BOOK OF)
ARIEL MOTORCYCLES 1933-1951 WSM
ARIEL PREWAR MODELS 1932-1939 (BOOK OF)
BMW M/CYCLES R26 R27 (1956-1967) FACTORY WSM
BMW M/CYCLES R50 R50S R60 R69S (1955-1969) FACTORY WSM
BSA BANTAM (BOOK OF)
BSA ALL FOUR-STROKE SINGLES & V-TWINS 1936-1952 (BOOK OF)
BSA OHV & SV SINGLES - 250cc 1954-1970 (BOOK OF)
BSA OHV & SV SINGLES 1945-54 250-600cc (BOOK OF)
BSA OHV SINGLES 350 & 500cc 1955-1967 (BOOK OF)
BSA PRE-WAR MODELS TO 1939 (BOOK OF)
BSA TWINS 1948-1962 (BOOK OF)
BSA TWINS 1962-1969 (SECOND BOOK OF)
CATALOG OF BRITISH MOTORCYCLES (1951 MODELS)
DOUGLAS PRE-WAR ALL MODELS 1929-1939 (BOOK OF)
DOUGLAS POST-WAR ALL MODELS 1948-1957 FACTORY WSM
DUCATI 160cc, 250cc & 350cc OHC MODELS FACTORY WSM
HONDA 50 ALL MODELS UP TO 1970 INC MONKEY & TRAIL (BOOK OF)
HONDA 90 ALL MODELS UP TO 1966 (BOOK OF)
HONDA MOTORCYCLES 125-150 TWINS C/CS/CB/CA WSM
HONDA MOTORCYCLES 250-305 TWINS C/CS/CB WSM
HONDA MOTORCYCLES C100 SUPER CUB WSM
HONDA MOTORCYCLES C110 SPORT CUB 1962-1969 WSM
HONDA TWINS & SINGLES 50cc TO 305cc 1960-1966 (BOOK OF)
HONDA TWINS ALL MODELS 125cc THRU 450cc UP TO 1968 (BOOK OF)
INDIAN PONYBIKE, BOY RACER & PAPOOSE ILL PARTS LIST & SALES LIT
LAMBRETTA ALL 125 & 150cc MODELS 1947-1957 (BOOK OF)
LAMBRETTA LI & TV MODELS 1957-1970 (SECOND BOOK OF)
MATCHLESS 350 & 500cc SINGLES 1945-1956 (BOOK OF)
MATCHLESS 350 & 500cc SINGLES 1955-1966 (BOOK OF)
NORTON 1938-1956 (BOOK OF)
NORTON DOMINATOR TWINS 1955-1965 (BOOK OF)
NORTON MODELS 19, 50 & ES2 1955-1963 (BOOK OF)
NORTON MOTORCYCLES 1957-1970 FACTORY WSM
NORTON PREWAR MODELS 1932-1939 (BOOK OF)
ROYAL ENFIELD 736cc INTERCEPTOR FACTORY WSM
ROYAL ENFIELD 250cc & 350cc SINGLES 1958-1966 (SECOND BOOK OF)
SUZUKI 50cc & 80cc UP TO 1966 (BOOK OF)
SUZUKI T10 1963-1967 FACTORY WSM
SUZUKI T20 & T200 1965-1969 FACTORY WSM
TRIUMPH PRE-WAR MOTORCYCLE 1935-1939 (BOOK OF)
TRIUMPH MOTORCYCLES 1937-1951 WSM
TRIUMPH MOTORCYCLES 1945-1955 FACTORY WSM
TRIUMPH TWINS 1956-1969 (BOOK OF)
VELOCETTE ALL SINGLES & TWINS 1925-1970 (BOOK OF)
VESPA 1951-1961 (BOOK OF)
VINCENT MOTORCYCLES 1935-1955 WSM

www.VelocePress.com

www.ingramcontent.com/pod-product-compliance
Lightning Source LLC
Chambersburg PA
CBHW070555170426
43201CB00012B/1853